B. Jan McCulloch
Editor

Old, Female, and Rural

Old, Female, and Rural has been co-published simultaneously as *Journal of Women & Aging,* Volume 10, Number 4 1998.

Pre-publication
REVIEWS,
COMMENTARIES,
EVALUATIONS . . .

"**T**his book highlights a group that has not received much attention in gerontology research and writing–namely, elderly rural women, whose resources and needs differ from those of urban women and of elderly men. The authors, all with experience in studying old rural women's lives, each focus on a different approach to the topic. From studying a single case to analyzing entire cohorts via census data, from focusing on access to health care to describing sources of informal social support, the chapters cover significant and timely topics. They illustrate the diversity that exists among this group and give evidence of strengths and effective coping strategies as well as problems such as poverty and isolation. This book should be of interest to gerontology researchers, educators, practitioners (especially in nonmetropolitan areas), and students as they seek greater understanding of old age from a rural woman's perspective."

Rosemary Blieszner, PhD
Depar
and (
Virgi
and ?

D1416480

More pre-publication
REVIEWS, COMMENTARIES, EVALUATIONS . . .

"**T**his collection explores the myths and realities of the lives of old rural women. Are they economically and health disadvantaged? Do they have supportive networks and strong ties to their communities? B. Jan McCulloch and the other contributors explore these questions and discuss the scholarly and practical implications of these divergent notions of older rural women's lives.

It is significant that this volume is written by women about women, because the topics included reflect the concerns both rural and urban women have about their future lives. McCulloch introduces the topic foreshadowing the five chapters that follow. Four of these chapters describe the realities facing older rural women, focusing on specific aspects of their lives. The final chapter is a summative one, written by one of the foremost authorities on rural gerontology, Vira R. Kivett.

One of the most important contributions of this volume is to highlight the diversity of older rural women's lived experiences rather than examining only what they have in common with each other. Sensitivity to this diversity should guide research designs, educational endeavors, and policy development."

Rebecca G. Adams, PhD
Associate Professor of Sociology
University of North Carolina
at Greensboro

More pre-publication
REVIEWS, COMMENTARIES, EVALUATIONS . . .

"**T**his edited volume examines in a thorough, scholarly, and creative manner, an important but much under-researched segment of the United States population–older rural women. Dr. Jan McCulloch has brought together the works of several well-known gerontologists who use diverse methods and approaches to begin to resolve the competing image of older rural women as 'mythical' strong, and enduring yet disadvantaged and vulnerable. Two of the papers (Drs. Shenk and Porter) use qualitative approaches (a case study and a phenomenological approach) to illuminate how older rural women negotiate their contexts during the aging experience. Using quantitative methods (a cohort analysis of a secondary data set and a longitudinal, theory-driven data analysis), Drs. McLaughlin and Scott examine the influence of labor force participation, marital patterns, familial relations and informal support on the economic well-being of rural women growing older. Finally, in a thoughtful and compelling synthesis of the above research articles, Dr. Kivett offers recommendations for future directions in research, policy making and education.

This timely collection of thoughtful research articles promotes our understanding of older rural women by combining the often forgotten perspective of the research participant with generalizable objective observations. The result is a well-written volume that will serve to enrich the understanding and background of graduate students and scholarly professionals."

Nancy E. Schoenberg, PhD
Assistant Professor
Department of Behavioral Science
Anthropology, Internal Medicine
and Sanders-Brown Center on Aging
University of Kentucky

"**T**his volume focuses on the realities of being old and female in rural America. The contributing authors rely on both qualitative and quantitative strategies to provide readers with insights into the multifaceted experiences of rural, older women. Collectively, the authors provide information about life and social circumstances that influence the women's daily lives. Dena Shenk uses a historical life review and network analysis to examine one woman's subjective evaluation of growing old in a rural area. Eileen J. Porter employs reflective dialogues with eight older women to better understand their experiences of accessing health care. More globally, Diane McLaughlin provides a detailed analysis of the economic situation of women aging in rural environments. Jean Pearson Scott examines changes over time in the informal support network of rural older women.

Each contributor to this volume puts forth a piece of the rural puzzle that Vira Kivett masterfully glues together in the final chapter. Kivett synthesizes the information covered and integrates the findings to provide readers with specific suggestions for future research, practice, and policy development. In the epilogue, McCulloch's concluding comments about the complexity of aging among this diverse group of women puts a frame around this picture of intertwined images of women aging in rural settings."

Karen A. Roberto, PhD
Professor and Director
Center for Gerontology
Virginia Polytechnic Institute
and State University

"**T**his volume fills a significant void in the gerontology literature. Its focus on the growing subgroup of older rural women provides insights into a segment of the population about which little is known. Dr. McCulloch has done an excellent job of bringing together experts from four different disciplines to illuminate the basic interdisciplinary nature of the field of gerontology. Similarly, the blending of four diverse research methodologies adds a dimension seldom found in one volume. Dr. Schenk's individual case study combined with Dr. Porter's larger qualitative study, Dr. McLaughlin's cohort analysis of 3 decades of census data, and Dr. Scott's regional longitudinal study provides a panoramic viewpoint from which to expand our knowledge about older rural women. Dr. Kivett's critique and synthesis together with Dr. McCulloch's introduction and epilogue expertly tie the four papers together into a very readable, thoughtful collection.

This volume confirms again that the older we get, the more diverse we become. Simultaneously, it points out that in the midst of our differences we share common experiences and qualities. Each of the chapters stands alone but each is enriched by its linkage to the others. The authors seek to broaden our knowledge about the realities of rural women's lives, especially their social support systems and general well-being in later life. Because of its ease of reading and the quality of the research presented, this book will appeal to gerontologists from diverse fields, academics in women's studies and research methodology, graduate and advanced undergraduate students, and professionals serving rural individuals and families."

M. Jean Turner, PhD
Associate Professor
Human Development
and Family Sciences
School of Human
Environmental Sciences
University of Arkansas

"**S**ince the 1980's rural areas have seen an increase in population resulting in a 'Rural Renaissance.' This volume represents a renaissance in the study of women residing in rural areas in the United States. Six researchers, themselves women, investigate the experience of growing old and female through a combination of qualitative and quantitative strategies. We see the humanity of these older women who try to control their lives under circumstances where networks are spatially dispersed and transportation can be problematic. Strong ethics of independence merge with the interdependency of kin, especially children, if they are available. Formal services are seen as a threat to self control and only are used once all other resources are exhausted.

One powerful message of this volume is the diversity in the social worlds of rural women. Staying 'close to shore' in familiar surroundings of place, family and friends, aptly describes these social worlds. However, how these women experience and define the social landscape is quite variable. Given migration and dispersal of friends and family, the social networks of these women vary and change through time. A sobering point, is that in comparison to their urban counterparts, rural women have had less opportunity to participate in the labor force. Consequently when they grow old, they are more economically disadvantaged. Without a history of wage labor, contributory pensions do not exist.

Diversity in experiences of living and growing old can present challenges to researchers who try to analyze life in any social context. This volume goes a long way in trying to synthesize what appears to be contradictory generalizations about the life of older women who live in rural settings. By using data from the U.S. Census to small-scaled surveys and even life histories, we have a better understanding of what it means to be older, and female in non-metropolitan America."

Christine L. Fry, PhD
Professor of Anthropology
Loyola University of Chicago

Old, Female, and Rural

Old, Female, and Rural has been co-published simultaneously as *Journal of Women & Aging*, Volume 10, Number 4, 1998.

Old, Female, and Rural

B. Jan McCulloch, PhD
Editor

Old, Female, and Rural has been co-published simultaneously as *Journal of Women & Aging*, Volume 10, Number 4, 1998.

The Haworth Press, Inc.
New York • London

Old, Female, and Rural has been co-published simultaneously as *Journal of Women & Aging*, Volume 10, Number 4 1998.

The development, preparation, and publication of this work has been undertaken with great care. However, the publisher, employees, editors, and agents of The Haworth Press and all imprints of The Haworth Press, Inc., including The Haworth Medical Press® and Pharmaceutical Products Press®, are not responsible for any errors contained herein or for consequences that may ensue from use of materials or information contained in this work. Opinions expressed by the author(s) are not necessarily those of The Haworth Press, Inc.

The Haworth Press, Inc., 10 Alice Street, Binghamton, NY 13904-1580 USA

Cover design by Thomas J. Mayshock Jr.

Library of Congress Cataloging-in-Publication Data

Old, female, and rural / B. Jan McCulloch.
      p. cm.
      "Has been co-published simultaneously as Journal of Women & aging, volume 10, number 4, 1998".
      Includes bibliographical references (p.) and index.
      ISBN 0-7890-0664-2 (alk. paper).–ISBN 0-7890-0671-5 (alk. paper)
      1. Aged women–United States–Social conditions. 2. Rural women–United States–Social conditions. 3. Rural aged–United States–Social conditions. I. McCulloch, B. Jan. II. Journal of women & aging.
HQ1064.U5039 1998
305.26′0973′091734–dc21
                                            98-44956
                                            CIP

INDEXING & ABSTRACTING

Contributions to this publication are selectively indexed or abstracted in print, electronic, online, or CD-ROM version(s) of the reference tools and information services listed below. This list is current as of the copyright date of this publication. See the end of this section for additional notes.

- *Abstracts in Anthropology*
- *Abstracts in Social Gerontology: Current Literature on Aging*
- *Abstracts of Research in Pastoral Care & Counseling*
- *Academic Index (on-line)*
- AgeInfo CD-ROM
- *AgeLine Database*
- *Behavioral Medicine Abstracts*
- *Cambridge Scientific Abstracts*
- CINAHL (Cumulative Index to Nursing & Allied Health Literature), in print, also on CD-ROM from CD PLUS, EBSCO, and SilverPlatter, and online from CDP Online (formerly BRS), Data-Star, and PaperChase. (Support materials include Subject Heading List, Database Search Guide, and instructional video)
- CNPIEC Reference Guide: Chinese National Directory of Foreign Periodicals
- Combined Health Information Database (CHID)
- Contemporary Women's Issues
- Current Contents
- *Family Studies Database (online and CD-ROM)*
- *Feminist Periodicals: A Current Listing of Contents*
- *Human Resources Abstracts (HRA)*
- IBZ International Bibliography of Periodical Literature
- *Index to Periodical Articles Related to Law*
- Institute for Scientific Information

(continued)

- *INTERNET ACCESS (& additional networks) Bulletin Board for Libraries ("BUBL") coverage of information resources on INTERNET, JANET, and other networks*
- MasterFILE: updated database from EBSCO Publishing
- *Mental Health Abstracts (online through DIALOG)*
- National Center for Chronic Disease Prevention & Health Promotion (NCCDPHP)
- National Clearinghouse for Primary Care Information (NCPCI)
- *National Periodical Library–Guide to Social Science & Religion*
- New Literature on Old Age
- *Periodical Abstracts, Research II (broad coverage indexing & abstracting data-base from University Microfilms International (UMI) 300 North Zeeb Road, P.O. Box 1346, Ann Arbor, MI 48106-1346)*
- Periodical Abstracts Select (abstracting & indexing service covering most frequently requested journals in general reference, plus journals requested in libraries serving undergraduate programs, available from University Microfilms International (UMI), 300 North Zeeb Road, P.O. Box 1346, Ann Arbor, MI 48106-1346)
- *Social Planning/Policy & Development Abstracts (SOPODA)*
- Social Science Citation Index
- *Social Work Abstracts*
- *Sociological Abstracts (SA)*
- *Studies on Women Abstracts*
- Women "R" CD/ROM, a new full text Windows Database on CD/ROM. Presents full depth coverage of the wide range of subjects that impact and reflect the lives of women. Can be reached at 1(800)524-7922, www.slinfo.com, or e-mail: hoch@slinfo.com
- Women Studies Abstracts
- Women's Studies Index (indexed comprehensively)

(continued)

Special Bibliographic Notes related to special journal issues
(separates) and indexing/abstracting:

- indexing/abstracting services in this list will also cover material in any "separate" that is co-published simultaneously with Haworth's special thematic journal issue or DocuSerial. Indexing/abstracting usually covers material at the article/chapter level.
- monographic co-editions are intended for either non-subscribers or libraries which intend to purchase a second copy for their circulating collections.
- monographic co-editions are reported to all jobbers/wholesalers/approval plans. The source journal is listed as the "series" to assist the prevention of duplicate purchasing in the same manner utilized for books-in-series.
- to facilitate user/access services all indexing/abstracting services are encouraged to utilize the co-indexing entry note indicated at the bottom of the first page of each article/chapter/contribution.
- this is intended to assist a library user of any reference tool (whether print, electronic, online, or CD-ROM) to locate the monographic version if the library has purchased this version but not a subscription to the source journal.
- individual articles/chapters in any Haworth publication are also available through the Haworth Document Delivery Service (HDDS).

Old, Female, and Rural

CONTENTS

ABOUT THE EDITOR

B. Jan McCulloch, PhD, is Associate Professor at the University of Kentucky in Lexington. She holds a joint appointment in the Department of Family Studies, College of Human Environmental Sciences, and the Sanders-Brown Center on Aging. Dr. McCulloch's research interests include older rural women's mental and physical well-being, rural aging, and the home-based work experiences of rural women. She is currently examining the relationship of psychological hardiness to depressive symptomatology among elders living in diverse residential settings. Her research has been published in the *Journals of Gerontology: Social Sciences and Psychological Sciences*, *Journal of Applied Gerontology*, *Journal of Aging Studies*, *American Journal of Family Therapy*, *Journal of Nursing Research*, and *Family Relations*. She has co-edited a special edition of the *Journal of Applied Gerontology* entitled "Poverty Among the Elderly in Rural America."

Introduction

B. Jan McCulloch, PhD

Older rural women often are portrayed in mythical terms–stoic, enduring, tenacious, and independent–terms that reflect Americans' romance with rural and frontier life. Over the past two decades, in both historical and social/behavioral literatures, scholarly interest in the lives of older rural elders has increased. As the body of literature has developed about this specific population subgroup, conflicting images about the realities of older rural women's daily lives have emerged.

On the one hand, when compared with their urban counterparts, rural elderly women are portrayed as economically and health disadvantaged. For example, when socioeconomic status is examined, several factors contribute to a rural disadvantage. First, rural women, compared with urban ones, are less educated (Lingg, Braden, Goldstein, & Cooley, 1993), and they are more likely to experience life long histories of limited employment opportunities (Fitchen, 1990; McLaughlin & Holden, 1993). Second, rural women who seek employment must compete for jobs that fall within a narrower range of occupations, have less chance of promotion, are more likely to obtain part-time employment and/or employment without benefits, and are affected more negatively by economic cycle fluctuations than women working in urban areas (Haney, 1982). Porter (1989) also notes that the economic disadvantage found among rural women, especially older rural women, is complicated by the large percentage of rural female-headed households (39%). As women age, they are more likely to live alone; a factor that further compounds the economic disadvantage noted for rural older females (Schwenk, 1991).

B. Jan McCulloch is Associate Professor, Department of Family Studies and Sanders-Brown Center on Aging, University of Kentucky, Lexington, KY 40506-0054.

This volume was presented in total as a symposium at the 1997 Annual Scientific Meeting of the Gerontological Society of America in Cincinnati, OH.

[Haworth co-indexing entry note]: "Introduction." McCulloch, B. Jan. Co-published simultaneously in *Journal of Women & Aging* (The Haworth Press, Inc.) Vol. 10, No. 4, 1998, pp. 1-5; and: *Old, Female, and Rural* (ed: B. Jan McCulloch) The Haworth Press, Inc., 1998, pp. 1-5. Single or multiple copies of this article are available for a fee from The Haworth Document Delivery Service [1-800- 342-9678, 9:00 a.m. - 5:00 p.m. (EST). E-mail address: getinfo@haworthpressinc.com].

To date, information remains inadequate about residential differences in older women's self-assessed health or activities of daily living (McCulloch, 1991; Richardson, 1988). Although rural and urban older women have similar rates of mortality and acute disease, rural women have higher rates of chronic conditions, such as arthritis, hearing and visual impairments, ulcers, hernias, and back disorders (Richardson, 1988). Rural women also are more vulnerable to death from breast cancer (Van Nostrand, Furner, Burnell, & Cohen, 1993). The impact of events such as the farm crises and the "bust" economy within extraction industries (e.g., mining and forestry) have increased the incidence of mental illness in rural areas–another health concern where rural women are likely to be disadvantaged when compared with those residing in urban areas because of differences in the rates of economic growth and the greater likelihood of appropriate mental health treatment in more metropolitan areas.

Other accounts, however, characterize rural women in more advantaged terms, noting their supportive networks and strong ties to community. Scholars have identified strengths among older rural women (Dorfman & Mertens, 1990; Shenk, 1987). Rural women, for example, demonstrate traditional rural qualities that increase their coping mechanisms for dealing with barriers to economic well-being, health care access, transportation, and other needs (Shenk, 1987). They also continue to fulfill important family and community roles. McCulloch and Kivett (1998) note the six roles that characterize the daily lives of rural women. Roles relating to family, including the roles of mother, grandmother, and sibling, consistently remain important. Kivett (1988) found that the rural mother-daughter interaction was more important than interactions among fathers and sons. Community and friendship roles continue to be a "natural evolvement of the rural experience" (McCulloch & Kivett, 1998). Shenk (1987), for example, notes that older rural women use their definitions of these roles to expand their supportive networks, especially when accepting support from more formal avenues. In addition, rural women maintain their community roles for reasons that differ from their male counterparts. Women report the need to be involved in organizations and natural helping groups as a way of expressing care while rural men note their involvement as the result of their sense of moral obligation (Patterson, 1987).

Older rural women remain a mythical, legendary population subgroup, with many conclusions regarding their daily lives based on descriptions of early pioneer and farm life. More current demographic and epidemiological data, however, provide avenues for clarifying our knowledge about women growing older in rural places. The purpose of this volume, therefore, is to discuss the relationship between divergent realities of older rural women and the effects these views have on the development of scholarship and policy. To accomplish this goal, contributors have addressed specific issues using a variety of methodologies. For example, two papers (Shenk and Porter) report studies using qualitative approaches to examine rural women's adaptations to aging in rural areas and their willingness to access health care–studies that provide an "up close and personal" account of individuals' experiences. McLaughlin and Scott, on the other hand, examine rural women's economic well-being and informal social support using quantitative methods–studies that use more distant lenses to examine how the patterns of labor force participation, marriage, and family integration and reciprocity affect rural women's aging.

The volume contains five papers: four that address specific issues relating to the realities of being old, female, and rural. Collectively, they provide information about rural women's economic well-being, intergenerational family relationships, health care and service delivery as well as health and long-term care concerns. A final paper (Kivett) synthesizes these specific topic papers with the purpose of providing integration across methodologies and substantive content as well as critical review and recommendations for future research, education, and policy.

In the first paper, Dr. Dena Shenk uses a case study approach to examine one older rural woman's subjective evaluation of growing old in a rural area. Shenk integrates information concerning Hilda's negotiation of her aging experience and includes her historical life review and a network analysis of her support systems prior to and after relocation to a nursing home. Perhaps the most fascinating aspect of Shenk's contribution is the irony that results from the complexities of her subject's commitment to life long values and her aging experience in rural Minnesota.

Dr. Eileen Porter's paper follows and addresses rural women's experiences of accessing health care. Dr. Porter uses reflective dialogues with rural women in Missouri to examine the importance of "close shores" in their willingness to seek services and medical treatment. She employs a life-world perspective as an overarching theme to illustrate the relevance of understanding health care utilization from the perspective of the persons seeking assistance; an approach that has the potential of illuminating factors that restrict health service use among persons living in rural settings.

The third paper, Dr. Diane McLaughlin's paper on the economic well-being of women aging in nonmetro (rural) areas, provides a detailed analysis of census data and compares the economic realities of rural women to those aging in urban environments. The use of census data provides the broadest view of the factors that contribute to rural women's later life financial well-being. The quantitative results forcefully indicate the complexity of estimating women's financial status in old age. In her conclusions, McLaughlin cautions that the retirement futures for older rural women–rather than being a time of increased economic stability due to more labor force participation—may continue patterns of historical disadvantage and financial hardship.

Dr. Jean Scott provides the fourth paper. She examines changes in the informal support networks of women aging in the rural southwest. Her sample, though small, provides longitudinal data for a group that has received limited study. Scott documents decreases in rural older women's help given to family as well as the important increases in help given by families as this shift in reciprocity occurs. In addition, she examines where these reciprocal shifts are most likely to occur as well as factors that predict help received by rural elderly women from their children over time.

Dr. Vira Kivett's paper, the final one in the series, provides a synthesis of the information covered in the first four. It is included to explicitly draw the reader's attention to the benefit of examining a group of papers in total, rather than as isolated pieces of information about a unique, complex population subgroup. Kivett pulls together the idiosyncratic experiences of single (Shenk) and limited numbers of rural older women (Porter) and the patterns identified by larger samples of women growing old in rural communities (McLaughlin and Scott) to identify similarities and differences across samples and methodologies. In addition, she integrates results across the papers to more clearly determine the implications for research, education, and policy.

The total set of papers, then, provides the reader with information on being female and growing old in a rural setting. Across a variety of settings, methodologies, and issues, the uniqueness and complexity of older rural women's lives are illuminated. And although they do not provide a definitive documentation of rural elderly women's experiences, they underscore the rich history, character, and life experiences of aging in rural environments. They also point to the importance of examining the diversity *within* this aging group. Some older rural women continue to be married and have the financial resources, family support, and adequate personal resources to remain in their residences of choice while others, for circumstances within and beyond their control, must relocate to residences or communities not of their choosing.

REFERENCES

Dorfman, L. T., & Mertens, C. E. (1990). Kin relations in retired men and women. *Family Relations, 39*, 166-173.

Fitchen, J. M. (1990). Poverty as a context for old age in rural America. *Journal of Rural Community Psychology, 11*, 31-50.

Haney, W. G. (1982). Women. In D. A. Dillman & D. J. Hobbs (Eds.), *Rural society in the U.S.* (pp. 124-135). Boulder, CO: Westview Press.

Kivett, V. R. (1988). Aging in a rural place: The elusive source of well-being. *Journal of Rural Studies, 4*, 125-132.

Lingg, B., Braden, J., Goldstein, A. A., & Cooley, S. G. (1993). Income, poverty, and education. In J. F. Van Nostrand (Ed.), *Vital and health statistics. Common beliefs about the rural elderly: What do national data tell us?* (pp. 25-31). (Series 3: Analytic and Epidemiological Studies, No. 28, DHHS Publication No. (PHS) 93-1412). Washington, DC: U.S. Government Printing Office.

McCulloch, B. J. (1991). Health and health maintenance profiles of older rural women, 1976-1986. In A. Bushy (Ed.), *Rural nursing, Vol. 1* (pp. 281-296). Newberry Park, CA: Sage.

McCulloch, B. J., & Kivett, V. R. (1998). Older rural women: Aging in historical and current contexts. In R. T. Coward & J. A. Krout (Eds.), *Aging in rural settings* (pp. 149-166). New York: Springer.

McLaughlin, D. K., & Holden, K. C. (1993). Nonmetropolitan elderly women: A portrait of economic vulnerability. *Journal of Applied Gerontology, 12,* 320-334.

Patterson, S. L. (1987). Older rural natural helpers: Gender and site differences in the helping process. *The Gerontologist, 27,* 639-644.

Porter, K. H. (1989). *Poverty in rural America: A national overview.* Washington, DC: Center on Budget and Policy Priorities.

Richardson, H. (1988). The health plight of rural women. *Women and Health, 12,* 41-54.

Shenk, D. (1987). *Someone to lend a helping hand: The lives of older rural women in central Minnesota.* St. Cloud, MN: Central Minnesota Council on Aging.

Schwenk, R. N. (1991). Women 65 years or older: A comparison of economic well-being by living arrangement. *Family Economics Review, 4,* 2-8.

Van Nostrand, J. F., Furner, S. E., Burnell, J. A., & Cohen, R. A. (1993). Health. In J. F. Van Nostrand (Ed.), *Vital and health statistics. Common beliefs about the rural elderly: What do national data tell us?* (pp. 25-31). (Series 3: Analytic and Epidemiological Studies, No. 28, DHHS Publication No. (PHS) 93-1412). Washington, DC: U.S. Government Printing Office.

Van Nostrand, J. F., Furner, S. E., Burnell, J. A., & Cohen, R. A. (1993). Social networks. In J. F. Van Nostrand (Ed.), *Vital and health statistics. Common beliefs about the rural elderly: What do national data tell us?* (pp. 25-31). (Series 3: Analytic and Epidemiological Studies, No. 28, DHHS Publication No. (PHS) 93-1412). Washington, DC: U.S. Government Printing Office.

Subjective Realities
of Rural Older Women's Lives:
A Case Study

Dena Shenk, PhD

SUMMARY. This paper presents and analyzes the subjective reality of a single older rural woman through her telling of her life story and open-ended interviews. This case study is used to demonstrate how a rural woman experiences a positive life experience while living with poverty, poor health, and numerous challenges and losses. The case was selected from the multiphase Rural Older Women's Project completed in rural Minnesota in 1986 and 1987. This representation shows the respondent living her later life and adjusting to old age in the same ways she has always faced life's challenges—with stoicism and tenacity, as well as patience and good humor. In the telling of her life story we recognize key values of rural older women including independence and privacy, balanced with a clear sense of the importance of relationships with others, and a closeness to the land. The views of informal and formal systems of service delivery are discussed and implications explored for the development of formal services which will more effectively meet the needs of rural older women. *[Article copies available for a fee from The Haworth Document Delivery Service: 1-800-342-9678. E-mail address: getinfo@haworthpressinc.com]*

Dena Shenk is Director of the Gerontology Program and Professor of Anthropology, Department of Sociology, Anthropology and Social Work, the University of North Carolina at Charlotte.

Address correspondence to: Dena Shenk, Department of Sociology, Anthropology and Social Work, University of North Carolina at Charlotte, Charlotte, NC 28223 (E-mail: Dshenk@email.uncc.edu).

[Haworth co-indexing entry note]: "Subjective Realities of Rural Older Women's Lives: A Case Study." Shenk, Dena. Co-published simultaneously in *Journal of Women & Aging* (The Haworth Press, Inc.) Vol. 10, No. 4, 1998, pp. 7-24; and: *Old, Female, and Rural* (ed: B. Jan McCulloch) The Haworth Press, Inc., 1998, pp. 7-24. Single or multiple copies of this article are available for a fee from The Haworth Document Delivery Service [1-800-342-9678, 9:00 a.m. - 5:00 p.m. (EST). E-mail address: getinfo@haworthpressinc.com].

Older rural women are often portrayed in mythical terms as stoic, enduring, tenacious, and independent. On the one hand, much has been written
about the increasing poverty, poorer health and declining opportunities in
rural areas (Glasgow, 1993; Scheidt & Norris-Baker, 1990). At the same
time, other accounts characterize rural women as advantaged, noting their
supportive networks and strong ties to the community. Kivett, for example,
notes that rural women benefit from a rich heritage of female friendship
networks (1990). These are not, in fact, conflicting portrayals but rather, they
emphasize different aspects of the rural aging experience. Both the negative
and positive characteristics are aspects of the life experiences of the rural
older women with whom I worked. The case I have chosen for this analysis
exemplifies this duality. In this article I will present the subjective reality of
Mrs. Hilda Lars[1] through her telling of her life story and my subsequent
interviews and communication with her. Through this case study, I will demonstrate how a rural woman experiences a positive life experience while
living with poverty, poor health, and numerous challenges and losses. This
perspective includes insights into the *cultural components* of life events and
personal circumstances (Murphy, Scheer, Murphy, & Mack, 1988). It also
illustrates the complex intertwining of individual character, personal and
cultural values and meanings (Deppen-Wood, Luborsky, & Scheer, 1997).
These factors pattern how individuals *interpret* life events and conditions of
life.

Hilda Lars' representation of her life story shows her living her later life
and adjusting to old age in the same ways she has always faced life's challenges–with stoicism and tenacity, as well as patience and good humor. She
explains that she and her husband have always been poor, life has been hard
and she has always been "sickly." At the age of 90, she and her husband
were continually adapting to the changes brought on by aging and the deaths
of friends and family members. They lived in their lifelong home, supporting
each other through 69 years of marriage, the death of both of their sons, and
increasing frailty. Her support system, however, was not able to sustain her in
this home when her husband died. In addition, she was unwilling to seek
support from the formal service delivery system because of her views of the
proper role of informal and formal systems of support.

WORLDVIEW AND VALUES

In Hilda's telling of her life story we find threads which reflect key values
of rural older women. These values include independence and privacy, balanced with a clear sense of the importance of relationships with others, and a
closeness to the land. She displays the common hope that her increasing
needs will be met by her informal network of family, friends and neighbors

and the related view that formal services are an approach to be used when one's informal network is unable to meet one's needs. She also displays great certainty about the appropriate roles for women in rural America both today and in the past, which are reflected in her descriptions of her own life. These women believe, for example, that women's roles are predominantly related to maintenance of social relationships and that appropriate tasks are defined by the men in the family. Some of these views and values will be explored in my presentation and analysis of Hilda Lars' life story.

Independence and Relationships with Others

The potentially contradictory themes of independence and interdependence with others were both dominant in the life stories of my respondents. Independence is a strong value that has been noted in other literature about rural communities (see Beaver, 1986; Salber, 1983). These women all believe that independence is maintained by obtaining any necessary support and assistance within culturally prescribed guidelines, turning first to family. In particular, they seek to limit their dependence on formal services, which they feel would deprive them of control over their lives, choices and decisions. Their independent spirits combine with involvement in close social relationships, which are necessary to survive in the rural environment. Marriage is the cultural ideal and for those who are married, their concept of independence includes their spouses. When they speak of independence, they mean independence of the household unit. Many moved to their husband's home, or followed him when his job required relocation. Like most women of their generation, they all assumed that it was the wife's role to follow her husband and support him throughout their lives.

Rural elders are often long term residents of their communities and generally derive the benefits of involvement in ongoing networks of exchange and informal support (see Kahn & Antonucci, 1981). There is generally an expectation by elders growing old in a rural environment that they will continue to turn to family, friends and neighbors (these categories may of course overlap) for support in meeting increasing and changing needs. Those who move to the area or "marry in" may always be considered newcomers by those who were born there. These variables clearly affect the expectations of specific rural elders for informal support in their later years, the nature of their informal systems of support, and their use of formal services to meet their needs.

Rural Older Women's Views of Formal and Informal Systems

The rural older women in this study view formal services as options to be used cautiously because a formal, bureaucratic structure is not their preferred approach to dealing with problems. These are proud, active women who are used to being involved in dynamic networks of social exchange, and many find it difficult to adjust as their needs increase and their abilities to do things for others is limited by their physical declines. But they do adjust and their relationships with others change; they can, of course, continue to provide emotional support for others, but eventually the kinds of instrumental support they can offer becomes limited. Each of the women grappled with this contradiction–in order to remain as independent as possible, they may have to become more dependent on others and even turn to formal services.

METHODS

Ms. Lars was one of the 30 respondents who took part in the multiphase Minnesota Older Rural Women's Project. This paper is based on the findings of that project undertaken between March 1986 and July 1987 in the rural four-county area of Stearns, Sherburne, Benton and Wright counties.[2] The project was completed in several phases including the collection of: (1) life histories, (2) social network and questionnaire data, and (3) photographs of the participants. A follow-up telephone survey was completed in 1990 to ascertain the ways in which their lives had changed in the interim. In the original project, each participant was visited in her home numerous times over a period of more than a year. The 30 respondents ranged in age from 62 to 93 at the beginning of the interview phase of the project. The sample was selected to include a broad range of participants in terms of key demographic variables. I selected the 30 participants based on both demographic guidelines and self-definition as a rural person. For further discussion of the methods and sample, see Shenk (1998) and Shenk and Christiansen (1997).

This case was chosen for analysis because of the respondent's clear sense of her own values and limits as she provided consistent descriptions of her life story and adaptations to life's challenges. Hilda Lars presented a rich life history in which she recounted her life beginning with memories from the age of two. Although she had less than a high school education and described herself as "quite common," she struck me as remarkable. I stayed in touch with Hilda until 1991 and can update her life story through her letters. In many ways she epitomizes the mythical older rural woman, and incorporates both a sense of adversity along with the advantages of aging in a rural community as she presents her life story.

THE CASE

Hilda Lars looked out the window of the farmhouse where she has lived with her husband since they were married in 1918, and talked about her life from her vantage point at the age of 90.

I was born at Winthrop, Minnesota. Then, when I was three years old, we moved to a large place near Gibbon, and we lived there for a few years. Not very long and we moved to Hasty. I was seven years old when my folks moved up here. So I went to school. . . . I always had to do a lot of hard work at home, because my mother was sick, very sickly. I could go to school one or two days, then I had to stay home one or two days and work, but I kept up my work in school just the same. So I got along. Of course, after, as long as I was home I worked like a man, because I was the oldest in the family. . . . But after I was married I never did any work like that. I used to do everything outdoors, excepting milking the cows. My dad wouldn't let me do that, because he said that I dried up the cows. So I had to feed the pigs and the calves. That was my morning and night chores. After I came here, I never had to do that. (My husband) always said that my place was in the house. For many years I boarded the teachers from the Hasty School.[3]

She described her life as "very common, a lot of hard work. I enjoyed everything. When we started out here (on the farm, when she married), that was 68 years ago." When asked to imagine her life as a story, she easily divided her story into three chapters. "The first chapter would be before we came up here"; moving with her parents to Hasty, Minnesota when she was seven years old. The second chapter would be "until I got married." The third chapter is "married life." Hilda then recounted her life story, beginning with memories of her second birthday. She and her husband were married when he returned from the Service in World War 1.

I promised him that if we both felt the same way after he'd be gone a year, then I'd marry him. He held me to that, and he came back from the service, we got married. He didn't get out until the next April. . . . He was in Texas. That was my daily prayer that he'd never have to go across, and the Lord answered that. He got back on the 7th of April. We came right up here. His mother was living here then. She went away. Her sister-in-law was going to Spokane, Washington to live. That's when we started here, and we've been here ever since. That was in 1918. Then Lemoin was born the 21st of February in 1921. And Bryce was born the 6th of March in 1923, so they were just two years apart. They were as different as night and day, just two years apart. The oldest one was just like his dad, exactly. The youngest one, I don't know who he was like. I suppose he resembled me more. He's the one who always wanted to help me in the house, and the other never wanted to do anything in the house. He wanted to be outdoors. We always had a very close family. We were very much attached to each other. I don't know, there was always lots of hard work. We had a lot of good times in between.

Both of Hilda's sons have died and she told me these stories with slightly teary eyes. Yet, she describes herself as a happy person and this is reflected in her story of her life, as well as her portrayal of her social relationships. She has made many new friends as her old friends have died.

> Well, I always enjoyed doing things. I always did. I enjoy being with all the people that were there. I never did do much of any work after we were married, that is, out away from home. My work was at home, big gardens. We had two boys. They're both gone. The oldest one died in 1947; he was 26 years old, and Bud died in 1983. He was 60. So we're left alone again, as we started out.
>
> We started out in this house. We've never moved. We didn't have anything, neither one of us. We were as poor as church mice, but that didn't bother us. Because we were happy as we went along. That kept us going, a lot of hard work.

Let's consider Hilda's life story in terms of the dual themes of adversity and advantages of rural life. Poor health and poverty were always a part of her life. At the same time, through adherence to such social values as independence combined with an emphasis on close social ties, she has lived a long, fulfilling life.

Adversity and Advantages

Hilda described her health as poor, stating several times that she has been "sickly" all her life. "I've been sick all of my life. Heart trouble, arthritis, and some gall bladder trouble." At other times she discussed her "poor heart," paralysis and broken arm. When the researcher asked her if there was anything else she wanted to add to the life story she had told, she responded:

> Well, I've been sick an awful lot. . . . When I was 15 years old, I was totally blind for, it must have been for two or three months. I could see if they moved a lamp in front of me.

> (*Interviewer:* Is that right? From what?)

> I don't know, unless it was from severe flu. I don't know. I had a terrible cold, what happened I don't know. Anyway, I wore glasses since then. My eyes are not the best, but I see fair. Of course, after I was married, I had gall bladder trouble. I was scared to death of surgery. Just mention

surgery to me, I got frantic. I suffer with that, get spells you know when I thought I was going to die. . . . I've had surgery five or six times for different things. . . . Then I used to have the flu so terrible. The first fall after I was married, I had that 1918 flu. . . . I pulled through, but after that until a few years ago, I'd have flu every fall and every spring. I'd be in bed for a week, maybe two, mostly two. I've been sick an awful lot . . .

She went on at great length describing her health problems throughout her life, although we would not generally think of someone who is still living in her own home at the age of 90 as sickly or in poor health. That is, however, how she views herself.

In addition, Hilda's early life was affected by her mother's illness, which required her to take off a lot of time from school. When she was 20 years old, she worked one winter in a nearby city, but left because her mother was sick. She explains, "I had to come home and help them at home. That's why I left. Otherwise, I suppose I wouldn't have left." So illness and sickness have always been a part of her life.

She describes her life as always being hard and explains that she has always been poor. When we were first married, we didn't have anything at all. We were poor but it didn't bother us, neither one of us. Some people, when they have less than others, they grumble and so on. We never did; we were satisfied with what we had. We still are. We haven't got it like most people got it, but I've never cared for that.

Hilda's subjective view of her economic situation is that they are better off in retirement than they were throughout their lives. I cannot provide an "objective" assessment of this perception, because Hilda was unwilling to divulge her economic situation. In fact, having told me in intimate detail about her life, friends and family, she was unwilling to indicate the range of her income, indicating only that Social Security was their main source of income. When we were talking about their current needs, she explained her view to me: "We don't have much, but we never asked for help. You hate to."

Throughout her telling of her life story Hilda acknowledges poor health, poverty and hard times. Her brother died from sinus surgery at the age of 21. Her younger son died in a car accident when he was 26. Her older son died when he was 60 of a cerebral hemorrhage.

He had gone out to dinner with his wife. When they returned about 10:00, and he went to bed, and he got a terrible headache. He asked his wife for a cold compress. She hadn't even come to bed yet. After just a few minutes he asked her to change it, because it was so hot. She realized that something was wrong, and called an ambulance. He was unconscious before the ambulance came. That was on a Tuesday night and he died on Thursday, but he never regained consciousness. (My younger son) was so young, he was only 26. He never had a chance to do the things that (my older son) did. (My older son) was so good to us. It was 4 years ago, but it's just like it happened yesterday.

She told me then about the deaths of her brother, father and mother. "I missed her terribly, but it wasn't like when (my older son) died." She recounts these as part of her story, but does not dwell on these challenges, all of which she presents as a natural part of life. In telling her story, she also portrays the advantages of aging within a rural environment. These include adapting to the transitions that come with aging through independence, along with a reliance on others.

Independence and Social Supports

Hilda lived alone with her husband in the farmhouse where she joined him when they were married. When I met her she was 90 years old and she was heavily dependent on the daily mutual support of her husband. She had a very close relationship with her 85 year-old sister who lived 20 miles away in a nursing home. She and her husband visited this sister about once a week. Her 80 year-old sister lived about 12 miles away. She explained that they called each other daily, but she was not as close as she was with her other sister. Her relationship with her nephew was important because he fixed their car. Hilda also had close relationships with her two daughter-in-laws and her one grand-daughter. She considered both daughter-in-laws to be very good friends and described her relationship with each of them in similar terms. She saw the daughter-in-law who lived in Minneapolis a couple of times a month compared to once or twice a year for the daughter-in-law who lived in Chicago. She exchanged gifts with both of them and talked with them both about personal things.

She had lived in the community for a very long time and close family, friends and neighbors helped to enable them to remain at home. She had numerous friends, including one best friend with whom she exchanged gifts on occasions. This friend provided rides occasionally and helped take care of her when she was sick. A younger neighbor plowed their snow—a crucial task in Minnesota.

> They keep an eye on us. He plows the snow from our driveway. They are available in case we need them, but we don't depend on them for anything in particular. We couldn't live here if it weren't for them.

Several of her friends' children visited her, as often as once a week. They provided rides, visited, and shared meals. She had a functional but fragile system of informal support.

Hilda was unwilling to turn to formal services for support and her knowledge of available services was limited. When we discussed whether she would ever use any formal services, she kept responding that they wouldn't come to her this far out. For example, she said she wouldn't use a van or bus service as long as her husband could drive. "There's no reason to use it and they probably wouldn't come out here anyway." She went on to explain, "We have a friend in Monticello who will drive in an emergency, so we can call on him if we need someone. But he works, so he's not always available." She was aware of County Home Health Services and, in fact, used this program when she broke her arm four years before. She explained:

> When I broke my arm, one (aide) came from Buffalo once or twice. Then the doctor sent one from Monticello. All she did was make sure I took my medicines (cynical laugh). That wasn't any good; I did that on my own. I needed someone to clean the house.

Perceived Needs and Adaptations to Aging

Hilda's major difficulty in adjusting to increasing frailty was cleaning and keeping the house the way she liked. She explained several times that her biggest problem on a daily basis was "Housekeeping. I can't keep house like I used to and that really bothers me."

> It's hard. Sometimes I'll see a cobweb. I can't sweep them down. My husband has to do that. He's older than I am and he's done his work. And I feel that it's too hard for him to do it. But I do dread the thought of going to a nursing home. It's wonderful that they have those places, but I hope that I never have to go there.

She was frustrated by her perceived inability to afford what it costs to have someone come clean the house, as she explained.

> My sister had one of those housekeepers from Social Services and it cost $9 an hour and the minimum charge was $27. Who could afford that? We can't. We also checked on some others, one was $10 an hour and another was $11 an hour. That is ridiculous, even at $9 an hour. We do need help with the housework the most.

Her husband had taken over the vacuuming, but didn't do it the way she liked. She was interested in getting someone to help, but felt unable to pay what she had heard it would cost and was unwilling to explore her eligibility for specific programs. She was very private about their finances, you recall. She stated: "I don't think that's anyone's business. We live nicely but we have to be careful. We can't buy everything, but we have all that we need." They did the best they could by themselves, rather than turn to formal services for assistance, which she feared would require them to disclose their financial situation and lose control of their lives.

There were numerous other ways in which Hilda and her husband had adapted to their increasing frailty and losses. They had outlived many of their friends, as she explained:

> Most of our friends are dead you know. We had a bunch of friends we got together with twice a month or so. We were the youngest of the group, so you know they're all gone. After that we made friends with people who moved up here. They're dead and gone now, so we had to make new friends.

I commented that some people found it difficult to make new friends. Hilda looked surprised and responded:

> That ain't necessary. We've made friends with lots of other people, lots of people. They're friends you know, but they're not special friends.

She listed a number of adaptations they have had to make. They don't go to church as much as they would like, and she explained:

> We rely on the television for our church services. I get dizzy in the morning, so I'm not able to go to the early service at our church. I don't go to the Legion Auxiliary meetings anymore, because they meet at night. We used to meet in the afternoon and I never missed a meeting, but (my husband) can't drive at night. We had to give up our Rebecca chapter, because we didn't have enough members, and I still belong as a member-at-large to the St. Cloud group. I went to the yearly meeting in St. Cloud last year. I was also very involved in the Ladies Aid at our church when there was one in Hasty. I was the president for 12 years. I was also a Sunday School teacher; I played the piano and organ. So I had lots of duties in the church.

Another adjustment to their decreasing energy was that this was the first year they hadn't planted a garden. This year they had only planted a few squash and tomato plants, and a flower garden. She explained: "Neither one of us can work in a garden and keep it up the way we like." At another time when we talked about this, her husband calmly stated: "There's a time for everything."

While each woman coped with the challenges she confronted in later life, for most of them old age was difficult. Due to economic limitations, the loss of members of their social networks, specifically the death of their spouses and friends, and the physical changes they confronted, the final chapters of their lives were fraught with dilemmas and difficult adjustments. Hilda Lars expressed her situation in the following words:

> It's hard getting old, in some ways. You have to learn to slow down. That was hard for me. I would forget, but I'd get up quickly from a chair and then I'd fall down. I used to be able to do so much, but now I can't. I just don't have the strength. I walk every morning. This is a diamond; I walk around and come back again. This morning I walked five times, that's almost a quarter of a mile. I do that twice a day, if we're home.

Like most of the women, she was calm and accepting of her situation. Hilda summed up her circumstances in the following words: "We're not getting along as good as we could, but we live one day at a time." She and her husband were facing difficulties in their old age, and wanted to remain in their own home as long as possible. She explained:

> We're not getting along as good as we could, but we live one day at a time. You know, to talk about the future would be impossible because one of us may pass on tomorrow. That's so sure that one of us is going before too long at our age. We want to live here as long as we possibly can, because here is where we've spent our life. And I'm afraid we wouldn't be happy anywhere else. I don't think we would. I suppose when it comes to where we cannot live here, our only thing we can do is to go to a nursing home unless we could get someone to come and stay here with us.

The Final Chapter

Hilda's husband died the following year when she was 91 and he was 92, and primarily because of her Parkinson's disease, she was unable to maintain her home alone. She moved to a nursing home on a "trial basis," but then sold her home and possessions. Although her friends and family continued to visit her, they were unable to provide the level of support required for her to remain in her own home. She had difficulty adjusting to this new stage of her life, as she expressed in the following segment from a letter:

> I have been at this Care Center for 3 years. It's like being in prison. The nurses and aides are so good to me, but it is still such a lonely place

and I can't seem to adjust to life without my husband. We had such a wonderful life together.

In December 1990, she wrote:

> After nearly three years, I still can't seem to adjust to being alone. There are 154 residents here, but it is the loneliest place. I have lots of company and get lots of letters. That's what helps me keep my sanity. My husband and I used to have so much enjoyment at this time of year, going to programs, parties and shopping. Wish I could do the things I used to do.

Several issues are confounded in these segments from her letters. Hilda missed her spouse with whom she shared her life for 69 years. She was also adjusting to life in an institution and dependence on others due to her failing health. She went on in a later letter to share that the "doctor was here to see me on Tuesday and told me I should live 20 more years. That bothered me, cause I'm old enough." She was confined to a wheelchair because of her Parkinson's Disease, dependent on the nursing home staff for her daily care, and unable to do much for herself anymore. This extreme loss of independence, along with the loss of her lifemate, left Hilda in a situation to which she could not fully adjust. She did not feel in control of the choice which necessitated her move into the nursing home, and knew that she had lost both her independence and her autonomy to make such decisions, and thus remain in control of her life. If she had been willing to seek support from social services, *might* she have been able to remain in her own home with the emotional support of friends?

Hilda Lars indicated her delight that the nursing home staff took her on excursions. She was frustrated, however, because she was unable to participate in such outdoor activities independently. She described her current activities in one of her letters.

> They have taken me along in my wheel chair to Como Park in St. Paul twice this summer and two weeks ago they took me along to Pirates Cove north of St. Cloud for a boat trip up the Mississippi. Which I enjoyed immensely. I climbed up way up on top where I could see good. Today they are taking me along on a picnic in a park by a beautiful lake. They take turns wheeling me in my chair.

After complaining about getting old being a headache, she ended with her usual upbeat, accepting attitude. "Think I better quit complaining and take each day as it comes." In this way, she retained her self-identity and positive attitude through her cheerful outlook and determination to accept life's challenges.

Each of my respondents sought peace and acceptance as they adjusted to life's changes. The loss of independence was difficult and left some of them depressed or confused. They found it difficult to adjust to the loss of balanced, reciprocal exchange relationships–the kind they were involved in throughout their earlier lives.

PROFILES AND MODELS OF SOCIAL SUPPORT SYSTEMS

Extensive network analysis profiles were developed for each participant through informal conversations, using a technique adapted from Sokolovsky (1986). Each participant was asked to talk about each person who was important in her life including: (1) community kin, (2) community non-kin, (3) non-community kin, and (4) other non-kin. Extensive data were collected regarding each relationship, including how long the informant had known the individual, how they first met, the nature of their link, and the things they did together and for each other. Finally they were asked to evaluate the importance of that individual to them.

A network chart was generated for each participant based on the data. The letter and number code of each individual on the chart refers to that individual's placement on the network analysis profile forms. A line connecting two individuals on the network chart indicates a close relationship between those individuals. The placement of a particular individual is based on the importance and depth of the relationship as described by the respondent. The respondent is charted in the center of the page and her closest family members and friends are those pictured nearest to the center. More distant relationships emanate out from the center toward the edges of the chart. These are generally described as second and third tier social relationships. Each member of the sample reviewed her own chart after it was drawn and made any adjustments she felt necessary.

Hilda Lars' network chart is reproduced here in Figure 1 with names replaced by relationships. Her support system was spouse-centered and dominated by a relatively small number of close family relationships. These few family members, plus a small but significant cadre of friends and neighbors provided crucial instrumental and emotional support.

I have come to imagine the various sectors of social support systems as balloons that must sometimes expand to fill the required needs or space. Balloons are expandable, but they sometimes break if stretched beyond their limits. In picturing a social support system, the size of each sector (i.e., family, friends, neighbors or service providers) is not a measure of the number of relationships within that category, but rather, is descriptive of the nature of the relationships within that category and how broadly they meet the individual's needs.

FIGURE 1. Hilda Lars' Network Chart

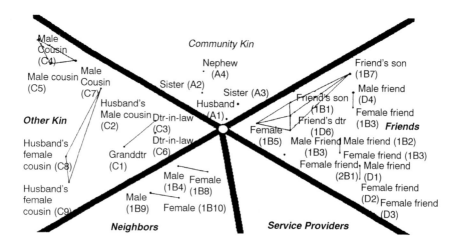

Using this approach we can consider Hilda Lars' system of social support, and assess the changes in her social support system after the death of her husband. Figure 2 represents her total system of social support while she lived at home with her husband. Note the relative size of the various sectors of her informal system of support and the total absence of any formal supports. Her family was clearly the strongest sector, although it was composed of relatively few specific individuals. Although there were relatively few members of her family sector, they fulfilled most of her instrumental and emotional needs with some support from her friends and neighbors.

Figure 3 represents Hilda's system of social support after her husband's death and her subsequent move to a nursing home. Comparing Figures 2 and 3, we see that her family sector shrank drastically when her husband died, because the remaining relationships were not able to expand to make up for the loss of this primary relationship. Her two sons had predeceased her, and her remaining closest relative was her sister who already lived in a nursing home. Her friends sector remained the same size, and you will remember, she noted that her friends continued to visit her after her move to the nursing home. She had several close friends with whom she exchanged gifts and occasional rides, but these relationships were not sufficient to meet her instrumental needs and enable her to remain in her own home. Due to her unwillingness to seek assistance from the formal sector to receive the support she needed, she felt forced to move to a nursing home.

FIGURE 2. Hilda Lars' Social Support System Before 1990

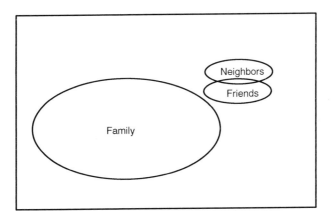

FIGURE 3. Hilda Lars' Social Support System After Her Move to the Nursing Home

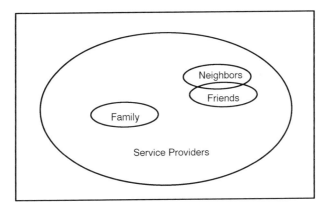

The irony, as pictured here, is that the formal sector now dominates her social support system, and she is dependent on the formal service providers in the nursing home. Her friends continue to provide emotional support through their visits, but the formal system of care in the nursing home has enveloped her informal social support system.

Discussion of Views of Formal Services

As we have seen in Hilda's case, these rural older women view formal services as an approach to be used when one's informal network is unable to meet one's needs. Hilda was wary of using formal services which she feared would draw her into a network of formal programs over which she would have little control. She viewed formal services as options to be used sparingly because she was not comfortable with the idea of accepting help from others and did not know enough about such a system to feel she could retain control. While she was in need of assistance specifically with housecleaning, she was unwilling to reach out to the formal system for this support. After the death of her husband, she found herself unable to continue to live alone. The support which was available from her fragile informal network was not sufficient and she had to move to a nursing home.

The formal service delivery system is based on the concept of replacing an unavailable or insufficient informal system of support with formal services. Rather than working effectively in cooperation with the informal support system, the formal system is often seen as a substitute for family and friends. The present framework of formal services and the existing service delivery system are largely unacceptable to rural elders who are in need of assistance to remain in the community due to their attitudes and expectations of what aging should be like. They are more likely to participate in programs and use services which meet specific needs without drawing them into an all-encompassing system of social services. Living in small communities where everyone knows everyone else, they are very concerned about public opinion and the impressions of their neighbors and friends. Ideally, rural older women would like to be able to pay for these services which, of course, they cannot always afford. This allows them to feel independent and in control and not to feel they are overly dependent on others. You will recall that independence and privacy are key values of these rural older women. As discussed elsewhere (see Shenk, 1998), our formal service delivery system is not designed to protect the privacy of those in need of services.

CONCLUSIONS

Much of the literature on the rural aging experience has focused on the dearth of services available in rural areas, the reasons why rural elders are underserved by formal programs and the problems caused by the unavailability of services. As we have seen from this case study, the present framework of formal services and the existing service delivery system are largely unacceptable to the rural elderly who are in need of assistance to remain in the community. Their rural attitudes and expectations of what aging should be like determine their approaches to meeting their changing needs. These women would much prefer to continue meeting their needs in old age as they have throughout their lives, through the networks of informal exchanges with family and friends. Turning to their informal systems of support allows them to retain their feelings of independence and privacy. Their values and attitudes related to independence and privacy, balanced with a clear sense of the importance of relationships with others, and a closeness to the land are central to their views of the world and expectations of old age.

The perspective which has been primary throughout this analysis is that of an older rural woman herself. Hilda's perspective represents a complex intertwining of her individual character, personal values and cultural values and meanings derived from the rural context. A second voice has been mine, the researcher who gathered, interpreted, and presented the research findings. These are both subjective views which I suggest are important to consider in conjunction with the statistical approaches that are often used to determine the needs of the rural elderly. The voices and views of rural older women themselves must be considered if we are to fully understand the rural aging experience, and we cannot ignore the diversity within the rural aging population. These views should be fully understood by the service providers and policy makers who are working with and on behalf of rural elders. It is only through an understanding of the perspectives of rural elders themselves that we can begin to understand their lived experiences and to develop programs and services to effectively meet their perceived needs.

AUTHOR NOTE

This research was completed in cooperation with the Central Minnesota Council on Aging. Financial support was provided by the Central Minnesota Council on Aging and St. Cloud State University through a research grant, Extramural Support Grant, Summer Research Stipend, and sabbatical leave and through grants from the St. Cloud State University Foundation, Central Minnesota Initiative Fund and Central Minnesota Arts Council. Thanks to Joel Savishinsky and Jan McCulloch for their thoughtful comments. With special thanks to the 30 rural women who made this research possible by sharing the stories of their lives.

NOTES

1. This is a fictitious name which is used to protect the anonymity of the respondent. My respondents shared their lives openly with the assurance that confidentiality would be maintained.

2. The project was completed with the cooperation and support of the Central Minnesota Council on Aging, the regional area agency on aging. The findings were

first presented in a report published by the Central Minnesota Council on Aging (Shenk 1987).

3. The oral interviews were recorded and transcribed word-for-word into computer files. The following annotational conventions have been used in presenting selected quotations from the interviews: ( ) explanation or replacement words provided by the author, . . . narrative text omitted from the original full text.

REFERENCES

Beaver, P. (1986) (reprinted 1992). *Rural community in the Appalachian south.* Prospect Heights, Illinois: Waveland Press, Inc.

Deppen-Wood, M., Luborsky, M. R., & Scheer, J. (1997). Aging, disability and ethnicity: An African American woman's story. In J. Sokolovsky (Ed.), *The Cultural Context of Aging: Worldwide Perspectives*, (2nd Ed.) (pp.443-451). Westport, CT: Bergin and Garvey.

Glasgow, N. (1993). Poverty among rural elders: Trends, context, and directions for policy. *Journal of Applied Gerontology, 12*, 302-319.

Kahn, R., & Antonucci, T. C. (1981). Convoys of social support: A life-course approach. In S. Kiesler, J. N. Morgan, & V. K. Oppenheimer (Eds.), *Aging: Social change* (pp. 383-405). New York: Academic Press.

Kivett, V. (1990). Older rural women: Mythical, forbearing, and unsung. *Journal of Community Psychology, 11*, 83-101.

Murphy, R., Scheer, J., Murphy, Y., & Mack, R. (1988). Physical disability and social liminality: A study in the rituals of adversity. *Social Science and Medicine, 26*, 235-242.

Salber, E. (1983). *Don't send me flowers when I'm dead–voices of rural elderly.* Durham, NC: Duke University Press.

Scheidt, R. J., & Norris-Baker, C. (1990). A transactional approach to environmental stress among older residents of rural communities: Introduction to a special issue. *Journal of Rural Community Psychology, 11*, 5-30.

Shenk, D. (1987). *Someone to lend a helping hand–The lives of rural older women in central Minnesota.* St. Cloud, Minnesota: Central Minnesota Council on Aging.

Shenk, D. (1998). *Someone to lend a helping hand: Women growing old in rural America.* Newark, NJ: Gordon and Breach.

Shenk, D., & Christiansen, K. (1997). Social support systems of rural older women: A comparison of the U.S. and Denmark. In J. Sokolovsky (Ed.), *The cultural context of aging: Worldwide perspectives* (2nd Ed.) (pp. 331-349). Westport, CT: Bergin and Garvey.

Sokolovsky, J. (1986). Network methodologies in the study of aging. In C. Fry & J. Keith (Eds.), *New methods for old age research* (pp. 231-261). Massachusetts: Bergin and Garvey.

"Staying Close to Shore":
A Context for Older Rural Widows' Use of Health Care

Eileen J. Porter, PhD

SUMMARY. Access to health care has been considered central to understanding older rural adults' utilization of health services. Access has been measured in terms of distance to care, use of care, and barriers to care; because older persons' relevant perceptions have received little attention, the validity of the typical access constructs is questionable. During a phenomenological study of their experiences of living alone at home, eight older rural widows shared perceptions about the locales where they received primary care and specialty care. A facet of their life-worlds, "staying close to shore," was seen as a frame of reference for their perceptions and as a general context for health care utilization. The implications of "staying close to shore" are discussed in relation to conventional conceptualizations of access. *[Article copies available for a fee from The Haworth Document Delivery Service: 1-800-342-9678. E-mail address: getinfo@haworthpressinc.com]*

Access to health care has been a particular emphasis in rural-urban comparisons of older persons' health service utilization (Bushy, 1993; Coward &

Eileen J. Porter is affiliated with the Sinclair School of Nursing, University of Missouri-Columbia, Columbia, MO.

Address correspondence to: Eileen J. Porter, S424 Sinclair School of Nursing, University of Missouri-Columbia, Columbia, MO 65211.

This research was supported by a Summer Research Fellowship and a Research Council Award from the University of Missouri-Columbia and a pre-doctoral fellowship, NIH/NCNR (NR06404-02). The assistance of Tracy I. Lanes, MSN, RN, is gratefully acknowledged.

[Haworth co-indexing entry note]: "'Staying Close to Shore': A Context for Older Rural Widows' Use of Health Care." Porter, Eileen J. Co-published simultaneously in *Journal of Women & Aging* (The Haworth Press, Inc.) Vol. 10, No. 4, 1998, pp. 25-39; and: *Old, Female, and Rural* (ed: B. Jan McCulloch) The Haworth Press, Inc., 1998, pp. 25-39. Single or multiple copies of this article are available for a fee from The Haworth Document Delivery Service [1-800-342-9678, 9:00 a.m. - 5:00 p.m. (EST). E-mail address: getinfo@haworthpressinc.com].

Cutler, 1989; Hicks, 1992; Lee, 1993; U.S. Senate, Special Committee on Aging, 1992). Although Salmon, Nelson, and Rous (1993) concluded that discrepancies in service access were greater across rural regions than between urban and rural regions, the typical conclusion has been that rural access is more limited (Coward, 1988; Hicks, 1992).

Most research about older rural persons' access has been designed to test regression models based on theories of health care utilization. The models' limited explanatory power has been attributed, in part, to the minimal consideration of variables influencing utilization (Benjamin, 1992). To reveal elements of experience that may not have been captured by scientific constructs (Husserl, 1913/1962), a descriptive phenomenological study was conducted concerning older rural widows' experiences of living alone at home, during which participants discussed their use of health care. The rationale for this descriptive work was derived from an analysis of the relevant literature.

REVIEW OF THE LITERATURE

The body of knowledge about older rural persons' access to care has been shaped in part by the Andersen (1968) model, which is the preeminent theoretical framework for the study of health service utilization (Burnette & Mui, 1995; Kart, 1991; Wolinsky & Johnson, 1991). Two key versions of the Andersen model exhibit somewhat different theoretical perspectives on access. In Andersen and Newman's (1973) description of the model, access was considered an influence upon utilization. Access, "the means through which the patient gains entry . . . and continues treatment" (Andersen & Newman, p. 102), was a component of the health care system. Access influenced the individual determinants of use, such as "accessibility to a regular source of care"–one of the "enabling factors [that] make health service resources available" (Andersen & Newman, p. 109). In contrast, Aday and Andersen (1974) viewed access to medical care as the outcome of interest. The "outcome indicators" (p. 216) of service use and consumer satisfaction were influenced by interactions among "process indicators" (p. 216) and system components including "entry" (p. 213). Aday and Andersen equated the system component of "entry" with Andersen and Newman's individual determinant "access."

As a potential influence on health care use, residence location also was conceptualized differently in these two versions of the Andersen model. Aday and Andersen (1974) considered "rural-urban" residence as an immutable, predisposing factor influencing the population's access. In contrast, Andersen and Newman (1973) considered the community's "rural-urban nature" as an enabling variable, due to potential urban-rural differences in medical practice norms or influential community values.

Although these distinctions between the Andersen and Newman (1973) and Aday and Andersen (1974) versions may have been complicating factors in defining and measuring access for older rural persons, an important similarity may have had a greater impact. In both versions, access was presented primarily as a component of the health system, but it also was portrayed in terms of personal resources, such as "accessibility" (Andersen & Newman, 1973, p. 109). This dualistic focus on access, which is evident in the two premier versions of the Andersen model, is also noted in both the survey literature and in research on older rural persons' health care use.

Survey Literature

Most scholars have emphasized the system-wide perspective, viewing access in terms of the health system (Light, Lebowitz, & Bailey, 1986), the rural region (Bushy, 1993; Krout, 1994), or both (Lee, 1993). Considering access as a person-centered issue is less common (Greene, 1985; Weinert & Long, 1987); Hicks (1992) described it as "the extent to which entrance into the system is reachable, obtainable, and affordable" (p. 23). It seems that other scholars have blended the personal and system-based perspectives; as predictors of access, Coward and Rathbone-McCuan (1985) cited "client eligibility, fiscal constraints, psychological constraints, and administrative practices" (p. 202). Distance has been considered a "major determinant of accessibility" (Coward & Rathbone-McCuan, p. 202), whether the focus is on access as a system component (Krout, 1994) or as a concern of older persons (Weinert & Long, 1987).

Research Literature

In research concerning older rural adults, three typical strategies have been used to operationalize the concept of access: distance to care, use of care, and barriers to care. Although distance was not highlighted in either version of the Andersen model (Aday & Andersen, 1974; Andersen & Newman, 1973), Ward (1977) said that it was an important enabling factor for older persons. Ward proposed that the Andersen and Newman model be reformulated to incorporate distance, but this has not been done. Medical geographers have been particularly interested in measuring distance to care; for instance, Love and Lindquist (1995) used the term "potential accessibility" to refer to "the locational relationship between service providers (hospital) and surrounding populations" (p. 633).

Rather than measuring distance to care, some scholars have operationalized the concept "realized access" (Hicks, 1992, p. 33; Love & Lindquist, 1995, p. 633) by counting the services older persons use, such as physician visits (Comer & Mueller, 1995; Wolinsky & Johnson, 1991). Gillanders and Buss (1993) simply considered service use as a proxy for access.

Finally, some researchers have measured access in terms of "barriers to service delivery" (Blazer, Landerman, Fillenbaum, & Horner, 1995, p. 1384), such as transportation and cost (Gillanders & Buss, 1993). These "barrier" variables are comparable to the "enabling variables" of the Andersen model. Among other variables, Wolinsky and Johnson (1991) considered the influence of geographic density, when they used the Andersen model to predict older adults' health care use. Aday and Andersen considered travel time as a "measurable variable affect[ing] initial entry into the system" (p. 217), but the individual's distance to care was not specified as an indicator of access. However, some researchers have operationalized access, in part, by measuring travel time to a health care facility (Gillanders & Buss, 1993).

Of the three constructs (distance, use, and barriers), none has been a particularly compelling measure of access (Hicks, 1992). Love and Lindquist (1995) noted that variables other than physical distance affect the use of health facilities, and they emphasized the importance of "individual preferences and perceptions" (p. 633) concerning access. For instance, the visibility (Magilvy, 1996) and acceptability (Coward & Rathbone-McCuan, 1985; Magilvy, 1996) of a service may be influential, as well as "differences in receptivity" or "potential psychological constraints" (Coward & Rathbone-McCuan, p. 205). To develop the knowledge base about access, exploration of older rural adults' perceptions and preferences about health care use may be a valuable strategy.

FRAMEWORK

Although more extensive study is needed of influences on older rural persons' service use (Krout, 1994) and access to care (Hicks, 1992), few scholars have explored older persons' relevant perceptions. Data on older rural persons' life circumstances are incomplete (Coward & Cutler, 1989); key contextual influences upon their use of health care have not been fully identified.

One such context is a person's "life-world" (*Lebenswelt*) (Spiegelberg, 1994). Constituted through social relations, the life-world is that "fundamental and permanent reality [that one] simply takes for granted" (Schutz & Luckmann, 1973, p. 3). The life-world "is an oriented world with an experiencing self at its center. Around this pole, the world is structured by such . . . patterns as 'near' and 'far,' as 'home ground' and 'foreign ground'" (Spiegelberg, p. 147). The life-world is comprised of component parts, or "objectivated categories" (Schutz & Luckmann, p. 180), which can constitute a taxonomy.

In a previous descriptive phenomenological study with older widows who lived in a community of 50,000 persons, I created a taxonomy to describe widows' life-worlds (Porter, 1995) undergirding their experiences of living at home alone (Porter, 1994). From general to specific, the taxonomic labels used to represent the life-world patterns were feature (Spiegelberg, 1994), descriptor, and element (Porter, 1995). The four features characterizing the widows' life-worlds were "knowing what living is all about," "being in the position," "facing vulnerability," and "living where I can best be myself." Each feature was composed of subsidiary descriptors, and each descriptor had its more minor elements, which were phrases summarizing participants' interpretations of important, routine life occurrences. For instance, a descriptor of the feature "being in the position" was "watching others watch me grow older," and one of that descriptor's elements was "being told what I should not do."

As recommended by Husserl (1913/1962), whose philosophy inspired my method, I used this preliminary work as a backdrop for further phenomenological investigation. The purpose of this study was to describe older rural widows' life-worlds as context for their utilization of health care. The specific focus of study was the widows' perceptions concerning the locales where they received primary as well as specialty care.

METHOD

To explore the context of experience, descriptive phenomenology is a particularly appropriate method (Husserl (1913/1962). The phenomenologist's chief goals are to identify what persons are trying to do with their experience and to ground this study in the person's life-world (Spiegelberg, 1994). Life-world data are revealed during reflective dialogue with persons about their experiences (Schutz & Luckmann, 1973).

Participants

The non-probability sample (N = 8) was recruited in central Missouri in 1996 through advertisements in local newspapers and notices in church newsletters. Consistent with a typical definition of rural persons (U.S. Department of Commerce, 1987), the women were non-farm, rural residents living in the open countryside (n = 3) or in a place with less than 2,500 residents (n = 5). They lived within 60 miles of Columbia (the region's city of 60,000 persons). The women had been widowed at least one year, lived alone, and had at least one child. The children of five women lived within 60 miles; the children of three women lived at least 200 miles away. Four women continued to reside where they had lived with their spouses; after the husband's death, the other four women had relocated. The women were of European ancestry and ranged from 75 to 84 years of age.

Procedure

At an initial home interview, informed consent was secured. Based on Spiegelberg's (1994) suggestions for investigating the life-world, a series of open-ended interviews was conducted with each woman in her home. The average length of the 23 interviews was 2 hours; on average, each woman had 3 interviews (range 2 to 4). Interviews were scheduled so that data were gathered from all women over the course of three months. Interviews were tape-recorded and transcribed.

Data Gathering and Analysis

Analysis was guided by a descriptive phenomenological method (Porter, 1994; 1995) based upon Husserl's (1913/1962) book, *Ideas,* and Spiegelberg's (1994) discussion of Husserl's unpublished writings about the life-world. Prior to data gathering, relevant literature was reviewed (as summarized previously); it was not considered again until the later stages of data analysis. Thus, participants were not asked directly about factors affecting their "access to health care." The initial stimulus for conversation was my request to "tell me what it's like to live here alone." I then asked for more information about the facets of daily life they discussed, including health care use.

The initial interview with the second participant was a particular influence on data gathering and analysis concerning health care use. Having always lived in a hamlet about 10 miles from Columbia, she said she had taken her father's advise that "little boats should stay close to shore." As we talked, I realized that "staying close to shore"–focusing her activities in and near a particular, familiar community–was a prominent contextual framework of her experience of living alone, influencing shopping habits and future plans, as well as her perceptions about using health care. Although the notion of "staying close to shore" was intriguing, I sought to avoid the bias of extensive reliance on first impressions (Huberman & Miles, 1994). However, the next participant volunteered similar data, noting that her community was "just here mostly." I then used this idea of "staying close to shore" as one focus for data gathering. As participants shared data pertaining to circumstances of health care use, I questioned them about services they considered "near" and "far." In this way, I explored the boundaries of their personal shores, particularly in relation to use of health care.

During their second interviews, I noted that participants repeated data concerning "staying close to shore," which I interpreted as evidence of confirmability (Lincoln & Guba, 1985). To gather further evidence of confirmability, I directly asked them, during ensuing visits, whether the notion of "staying close to shore" was relevant to them. Based on their reactions to the idea, I concluded that it was credible (Lincoln & Guba, 1985).

The primary analysis strategies were comparing data within and across interviews and drawing inferences (Husserl, 1913/1962). Life-world data were differentiated from data pertaining to the experience of living alone; the former were viewed as the background of or rationale for what the women were trying to do as they lived alone (Porter, 1995). For instance, for the woman who was described previously, a key aspect of living alone at home was "reducing my risks" by "placing restrictions on doing and going." She drove only to "town" (a community of 2,500 persons about 10 miles away). Driving an old car, she consolidated her visits to her primary physician with grocery shopping. "I was running short on eggs, so when I went to [town] to the doctor, I stopped and got eggs and frozen orange juice, what I needed, and took it on home." Although "it might cost me less to drive to Columbia," she had no plans to switch to a primary physician there or to buy groceries where she "would have to walk 10 miles down those aisles." It seemed that for her, a central life-world element was "expecting to get it all done in one easy trip."

In descriptive phenomenological analysis, the relationships among the component parts of the life-world (or the experience) must be characterized. As noted previously, an understanding of life-world can be represented with the taxonomic labels of element, descriptor (Porter, 1995), and feature (Spiegelberg, 1994). As shall be explained, older rural widows' perceptions about health care use were found to be particularly relevant to one life-world feature from the previous study with urban widows. Because the results of phenomenological study are never complete (Husserl, 1913/1962), the taxonomy of this feature was expanded to incorporate findings from the rural widows. Finally, the literature pertaining to access was re-considered in relation to the findings.

FINDINGS

With regard to health care utilization, "staying close to shore" was seen as a general context of the older rural widows' experiences of living alone at home. "Shore" was understood as the location of greatest familiarity, where the woman had a personal history and some social ties. Data pertaining to involvement with primary care providers and medical specialists reflected the influence of "staying close to shore" on health service use.

Results are described first for women who had not relocated after widowhood, followed by a description of results for women who had relocated after widowhood.

Four Life-Long Residents of Rural Communities

For their entire lives, three of these women had lived in or near a community of less than 1,000 persons–a place where "you can't get much." Their primary physicians practiced in a town about 10 miles away; this community of about 2,500 people was part of each woman's shore. When they went anywhere, that was their likely destination. They had some ties there; at least, they knew some merchants and health care providers. Even for the two women who did not drive, the distance to town was not an issue; family members who provided transportation used other services in town during those trips.

These women also had about a 10-mile trip to their specialists in Columbia. In contrast to their familiarity with the town of 2,500 persons, the women felt differently about Columbia, especially its newer regions. For the two women who did not drive, findings were similar, so data are presented about one woman, who said this about her primary physician's referral to a specialist:

> Now Dr. Richards, if there is something wrong that he doesn't feel like he could take care of, then he sends us to Dr. Simon in Columbia. Well, one time in the ER, Dr. Simon wasn't available and Dr. Dellwood came in; I liked him and he's over here by [a specific discount store]. And Dr. Simon is way out there . . . on Harrison, *way* out there. I hate to ask somebody to drive way out there to take me.

Although she often sent her daughters to that particular discount store (on Columbia's outskirts and on their "side of town"), the family rarely went to Dr. Simon's part of town. The family's familiarity with these two regions of the city influenced the woman's perceptions about access to specialists; one was "over here" and the other was "out there." Some elements of her life-world were "living in a place where you can't get much," "considering a place as far from home," "knowing that they aren't sure where we are when we're out here," and "preferring to go 'over here' rather than 'out there.'"

The third long-time resident of this hamlet shared the life-world elements of "living in a place where you can't get much" and "considering a place as far from home." Although she readily drove to town to see her primary physician, she was not comfortable driving to Columbia to see her heart specialist "way, way down on Harrison, or somewhere down there. Like my sister says, 'When you go that far, you might as well go to Kansas City'" [90 miles]. Previously, her Columbia specialist had "installed a young doctor in [the nearby town]. When he was there, I didn't go to Columbia. But then, he up and flew the coop, and they got nobody to replace what he was doing." Her reference to the chickens' house, or "coop," is consistent with her perception that when specialty care was provided in town, it was provided close to home–close to shore. Against this life-world context, her experience of living at home alone was structured, in part, by "negotiating reliance,"specifically by "hiring someone to take me that far." When the specialist left her hamlet, she again had to hire a driver to take her to Columbia for care.

One woman had always lived in a town of about 2,500, where she obtained primary care. Although her "heart and soul" were "right here," where her two sons and their families managed her farm, she drove the 30 miles to Columbia several times a month for activities with friends, to visit her daughter, or to see her specialist. She was "not thrown" by finding the way to the specialist's office, although she was "more used to" the area near her daughter's home. Her perception that the city was not so far from shore was evident in her disbelief that "there's such a long-distance rate between here and Columbia."

Four Women Who Had Relocated from Other Communities

Upon retirement (about 15 years prior to the interviews), one woman and her husband had relocated from a metropolitan area to a rural home about 10 miles from Columbia. She lived in her rural home during the "warm seasons," returning in the fall to her urban apartment in another state, where she lived a few blocks from one of her children. Her rural home was just a mile from the hamlet where the three life-long residents lived, but compared to them, she had very different patterns of service use. When she and her husband relocated, "All of our contacts were in Columbia." Of the town of 2,500, where the other three women purchased goods and obtained primary care, she said, "They don't have the things a person needs." She drove to Columbia for "everything except my mail," and she planned to sell her rural home "when I can't drive to Columbia anymore." In her case, the two nearby, smaller communities were "foreign ground."

Another woman, who lived in the country near her daughter for the past two years, had moved there when a flood destroyed her home. To see her primary physician every three months, she drove 90 miles to her former community. "I don't drive in the city; I was always a country driver. Going into Columbia, I haven't done that yet." She agreed that the familiarity of the trip to her former community "had something to do with" her readiness to drive 90 miles for a check-up. "[I'm] So used to it," she said. "I go right out here and go to Brighton and I take E right up to N and then take N to 22 and go through Eaton and then hit 84 and that brings you right up." She continued to obtain primary care on "home ground." Her life-world was patterned by "staying close to shore."

After her husband's death, another woman had moved from a city of 10,000 to a rural home near the small town where her children had grown up. Having related initially to her rural church and with relatives in the town of 500 about five miles away, she now related primarily to Columbia (10 miles away). "If I need any groceries on sale, then that's where I go. And of course, that's where my doctors are and there's where my boyfriend lives." Her familiarity with Columbia had been enhanced by two unique life-world elements: "being thought of by the kids as someone who could never drive in the city" and "being my boyfriend's designated driver." "Ya," she said, "that boyfriend's got me behind the wheel, and I can go everywhere now." She noted that her perception about what was "far from home" had changed during the two years since her move. "Here I thought I'd never get used to nine miles, but now it don't seem like it's far."

About two years prior to the interviews, the fourth woman had left a town of 20,000, moving 15 miles away to a hamlet of about 300 persons. "Everybody who lives here relates to [the town of 20,000]," where she saw her primary provider and specialist. Having "worked in Columbia and gone there to school for one session," she considered it "part of my big community." Sometimes she drove the 60 miles there alone, when she had special tests. Since her husband's death, she had undertaken various "adventures"–creative work, teaching, traveling, and volunteering. Although her life-world was not reflective of "staying close to shore," she immediately recognized its relevance for the lives of some acquaintances in her town and nearby rural communities. "And I'm amazed at the small world–of the very small world circumference of some of the ladies that I have contact with. They've never been here or they've never been there, and it's just a few miles away. And they don't know what it would be like."

As analysis progressed, I envisioned "staying close to shore" as a life-world descriptor; thus, it was located at the intermediate level of the taxonomy (element, descriptor, and feature) (Porter, 1995). It comprised several basic elements, such as "expecting to get it all done in one easy trip." "Staying close to shore" was a component of the broad, life-world feature, "being in the position," which I had described in the previous study with urban widows (Porter, 1995). Accordingly, for this rural sample, the taxonomy for this life-world feature (Porter, 1995) was modified, as shown in Table 1.

I envisioned integral relationships between the life-world descriptor, "staying close to shore," and other descriptors of the broader life-world feature "being in the position." For instance, the woman whose children had

TABLE 1. Revised Taxonomy of the Life-World Feature: "Being in the Position"

A. *Having my own time*
    1. not being time-scheduled
    2. letting myself have my own time
    3. turning things over (to younger persons)

B. *Being a valued member* (of families and organizations)

C. *Watching others watch me grow older*
    1. being told what I should not do
    2. having privileges

D. *Holding on and letting go* (of occupations, persons, activities, and objects)

E. *Staying close to shore*
    1. expecting to get it all done in one easy trip
    2. living in a place where you can't get much
    3. considering a place as far from home
    4. preferring to go "over here" rather than "out there"
    5. knowing that they aren't sure where we are when we're out here
    6. being a country driver
    7. being thought of by the kids as someone who could never drive in the city
    8. being my boyfriend's designated driver
    9. knowing women who have a "small world circumference"

been convinced that she would not become a city driver was in the position of "watching others watch me grow older"–even as she reconfigured the boundaries of her shore. For most of the women, "staying close to shore" was related to the position of "being a valued member" of a family. The women who were not city drivers and had to travel to see a specialist generally were assisted by nearby family members, with whom they shared a sense of "shore." While staying close to shore, the women who drove were in the position of "holding on [to driving in some situations] and letting go [of it in other situations]." For instance, the woman who considered Columbia as her shore, but had no family nearby, had decided she would leave the area when she could no longer drive.

DISCUSSION

For each of these rural women, "staying close to shore" had unique relevance as a life-world descriptor, because each woman brought singular life experiences to the designation of her own shore. Some women, particularly those who were life-long residents of tiny communities, had well-established and comparatively narrow parameters of shore, while women who had relocated, particularly those with some prior urban experiences, had a more open conceptualization of their familiar place. The range of nuances in this life-world descriptor is consistent with the heterogeneity of older adults.

With regard to access to health care and health care use, the findings are springboards for dialogue about some interesting issues. The life-worlds of these older rural women influenced their perceptions about the locales where they obtained health care. Perceptions about differences in the locales of primary care and specialty care were influenced by their views of what constituted "home ground" and "foreign ground."

It seemed that the participants' perceptions about access to care were related to their familiarity with the locale in which care was delivered. The women who had not actively moved about in the urban locales (i.e., had not driven there) described themselves as unfamiliar with those locales; they considered such places as "far from home." Although the actual distance to the urban locale was not great, it was perceived as far. The interaction of distance and perceptions about distance is particularly evident in the case of the woman who intended to move permanently to her urban apartment when she could no longer drive. Columbia was now her familiar shore but because it was not in her immediate vicinity, getting there would become problematic.

For the three women whose shore was confined to the very small communities where they had always lived, there were different ambiances associated with receiving primary care in a familiar, small town close to home and receiving specialty care in the unfamiliar, larger city. Two rural women, who had previously lived in urban areas, traveled to larger cities where they saw both primary and specialty physicians; they did not reveal distinct perceptions about the distance associated with primary care access and specialty care access. In this way, their life-worlds were comparable to the urban-dwelling women in the previous study (Porter, 1994; 1995), who had obtained both primary and specialty care in the same community.

In the literature, very little attention has been paid to familiarity with the care locale as a perception that may influence access to care. Older rural persons' familiarity with urban locales of care may be particularly important in an era of continuing interdependence of rural and urban populations (Watkins & Watkins, 1985). Because they are likely to receive their specialty care in urban environments, it is problematic to characterize them primarily as recipients of care in rural areas (Coward & Rathbone-McCuan, 1985) or to emphasize their limited knowledge of rural services (Krout, 1994).

Solutions to the "problem" of access are typically linked to a specific conceptualization of access. When it is interpreted as a personal resource, the problem may be viewed as the older person's resistance to seeking care (Cutler & Rathbone-McCuan, 1985); proposed solutions may be to enhance the visibility of rural programs (Krout, 1994). When access is interpreted as a systems-related problem, such as distance to care, then the typical proposal is to increase transportation opportunities (Krout, 1994).

This study is an impetus to reconsider the standard conceptualizations of access as either a personal resource or a component of the health system (Aday & Andersen, 1974; Andersen & Newman, 1973). Instead, it may be useful to understand access in terms of person-environment interaction. Perhaps older persons' perceptions about their access to health care cannot be divorced from their perceptions about their life-worlds. Based on an appraisal of the interrelated nature of variables affecting access, Coward and Rathbone-McCuan (1985) came to a similar conclusion, noting that attitudes, such as receptivity to a service, "interact with contextual variables like availability and accessibility" (p. 205).

If access is considered as a feature of person-environment interaction, then new approaches to labeling problems and proposing solutions are undergirded. Understanding access in terms of person-environment interaction enables consideration of older persons' unique perceptions about health care access and suggests the need for clients and providers to work together to enhance access. Recommendations to enhance older rural persons' access (Gillanders & Buss, 1993) have not focused upon increasing their familiarity with urban areas. If perceptions about access are functions of distance as well as familiarity (and other factors), then researchers and providers may be able to influence older rural persons' perceptions of what is "far from home" and so, enhance their familiarity with urban care locales. In terms of a person's *experience* of residence location, rural-urban residence may not be the immutable influence on health care access that Aday and Andersen (1974) described.

As the factors affecting older rural persons' perceptions are uniquely individual, interventions to enhance familiarity with care locales must be grounded in one-on-one interaction. Older rural widows must be given an opportunity to describe their own "shores," explain the extent to which it is important to them to stay close to shore, and share just how far from shore they are when they come to see the provider. For older rural widows who live alone, there may be more to understanding access than appraising distance to care, monitoring utilization, or ascertaining barriers to service. As Gillanders and Buss (1993) noted, "access . . . includes many dimensions" (p. 351). The experiences of older rural persons are a vital source of knowledge about these dimensions of access.

REFERENCES

Aday, L. A., & Andersen, R. (1974). A framework for the study of access to medical care. *Health Services Research, 9*, 208-220.

Andersen, R.M. (1986). *A behavioral model of families' use of health services* (Research Series 25). Chicago, IL: The University of Chicago Center for Health Administration Studies.

Andersen, R., & Newman, J. F. (1973). Societal and individual determinants of medical care utilization in the United States. *Milbank Memorial Fund Quarterly, 51*, 95-124.

Benjamin, A. E. (1992). An overview of in-home health and supportive services for older persons. In M. G. Ory & A. P. Duncker (Eds.), *In-home care for older people* (pp. 9-52). Newbury Park, CA: Sage.

Blazer, D. G., Landerman, L. R., Fillenbaum, G., & Horner, R. (1995) Health services access and use among older adults in North Carolina: Urban vs. rural residents. *American Journal of Public Health, 85*, 1384-1390.

Burnette, D., & Mui, A. C. (1995). In-home and community-based service utilization by three groups of elderly Hispanics: A national perspective. *Social Work Research, 19*, 197-206.

Bushy, A. (1993). Rural women: Lifestyle and health status. *Rural Nursing, 28*, 187-197.

Comer, J., & Mueller, K. (1995). Access to health care: Urban-rural comparisons from a Midwestern agricultural state. *The Journal of Rural Health, 11*, 128-136.

Coward, R. T. (1988). Aging in the rural United States. In E. Rathbone-McCuan & B. Havens (Eds.), *North American elders: United States and Canadian perspectives* (pp. 161-178). New York: Greenwood Press.

Coward, R. T., & Cutler, S. J. (1989). Informal and formal health care systems for the rural elderly. *HSR: Health Services Research, 23*, 785-806.

Coward, R. T., & Rathbone-McCuan, E. (1985). Delivering health and human services to the elderly in rural society. In R. T. Coward & G. R. Lee (Eds.), *The elderly in rural society: Every fourth elder* (pp. 197-222). New York: Springer.

Gillanders, W. R., & Buss, T. F. (1993). Access to medical care among the elderly in rural Northeastern Ohio. *The Journal of Family Practice, 37*, 349-355.

Greene, J. A. (1985). Health care for older citizens: Overcoming barriers. *Journal of the Tennessee Medical Association*, 289-293.

Hicks, L. (1992). Access and utilization: Special populations–special needs. *Rural Health Care*, 20-35.

Huberman, A. M., & Miles, M. B. (1994). Data management and analysis methods. In N. K. Denzin & Y. S. Lincoln (Eds.), *Handbook of qualitative research* (pp. 428-444). Thousand Oaks, CA: Sage.

Husserl, E. (1962). *Ideas: General introduction to pure phenomenology* (W. R. B. Gibson, Trans.). New York: Macmillan. (Original work published 1913.)

Kart, C. S. (1991). Variation in long-term care service use by aged Blacks: Data from the Supplement on Aging. *Journal of Aging and Health, 3*, 511-526.

Krout, J. A. (1994). Epilogue. In J. A. Krout (Ed.), *Providing community-based service to the rural elderly* (pp. 267-276). Thousand Oaks: Sage.

Lee, H. J. (1993). Rural elderly individuals: Strategies for delivery of nursing care. *Rural Nursing, 28*, 219-230.

Light, E., Lebowitz, B. D., & Bailey, F. (1986). CMHC's and elderly services: An analysis of direct and indirect services and service delivery sites. *Community Mental Health Journal, 22*, 294-302.

Lincoln, Y., & Guba, E. (1985). *Naturalistic inquiry.* Beverly Hills, CA: Sage.

Love, D., & Lindquist, P. (1995). The geographical accessibility of hospitals to the aged: A geographic information systems analysis within Illinois. *HSR: Health Services Research, 29*, 629-651.

Magilvy, J. K. (1996). The role of rural home- and community-based services. In G. D. Rowles, J. E. Beaulieu, & W. W. Myers (Eds.), *Long-term care for the rural elderly* (pp. 64-84). New York: Springer.

Porter, E. J. (1994). Older widows' experience of living alone at home. *Image: Journal of Nursing Scholarship, 26*, 19-24.

Porter, E. J. (1995). The life-world of older widows: The context of lived experience. *Journal of Women & Aging, 7*(4), 31-46.

Salmon, M. A. P., Nelson, G. M., & Rous, S. G. (1993). The continuum of care revisited: A rural perspective. *The Gerontologist, 33*, 658-666.

Schutz, A., & Luckmann, T. (1973). *The structures of the life world.* Evanston, IL: Northwestern University Press.

Spiegelberg, H. (1994). *The phenomenological movement: A historical introduction* (3rd ed.). The Hague: Martinus Nijhoff.

U. S. Department of Commerce, Bureau of the Census (1987). *Census of population, 1980: Vol. 1, Characteristics of the population: General social and economic characteristics.* Washington, D.C.: Government Printing Office.

U. S. Senate, Special Committee on Aging. (1992). *Common beliefs about the rural elderly: Myth or fact?* (Serial No. 102-N). Washington, DC: Government Printing Office.

Ward, R. A. (1977). Services for older people: An integrated framework for research. *Journal of Health & Social Behavior, 18*, 61-70.

Watkins, D. A., & Watkins, J. M. (1985). Policy development for the elderly: Rural perspectives. In R. T. Coward & G. R. Lee (Eds.), *The elderly in rural society: Every fourth elder* (pp. 223-241). New York: Springer.

Weinert, C., & Long, K. A. (1987). Understanding the health care needs of rural families. *Family Relations, 36*, 450-455.

Wolinsky, F. D., & Johnson, R. J. (1991). Use of health services by older adults. *Journal of Gerontology: Social Sciences, 46*, S345-S357.

Rural Women's Economic Realities

Diane K. McLaughlin, PhD

SUMMARY. The economic position of many elders has improved over the past few decades. Several groups of elders remain disadvantaged, however, including nonmetropolitan elders and women in any setting. This study examines differences in household income and poverty rates for metropolitan and nonmetropolitan women ages 55 and over in 1970, 1980 and 1990. Comparison of median incomes for women the same age across birth cohorts reveals that much of the improvement in women's economic well-being occurs because younger cohorts have higher incomes when they enter older ages. There also is evidence that incomes decline as the cohort ages. Nonmetro women have lower incomes and higher poverty rates than metro women in every comparison, even when demographic characteristics are controlled. While the metro/nonmetro income gap declines from 1970 to 1980, it increases from 1980 to 1990. The largest income gap occurs for women ages 55 to 64 in 1990, the youngest cohort examined, offering no evidence to support convergence of household incomes among metro and nonmetro older women in the near future. *[Article copies available for a fee from The Haworth Document Delivery Service: 1-800-342-9678. E-mail address: getinfo@ haworthpressinc.com]*

Diane K. McLaughlin is affiliated with Department of Agricultural Economics and Rural Sociology, and Population Research Institute, The Pennsylvania State University.

Support for this research was provided by a grant from the National Institute on Aging (RO1-AG11240). Institutional support was provided by the Population Research Institute, The Pennsylvania State University, which has core support from the National Institute of Child Health and Human Development (P30-HD28263), and from The Pennsylvania State University Agricultural Experiment Station Research Project (3548).

[Haworth co-indexing entry note]: "Rural Women's Economic Realities." McLaughlin, Diane K. Co-published simultaneously in *Journal of Women & Aging* (The Haworth Press, Inc.) Vol. 10, No. 4, 1998, pp. 41-65; and: *Old, Female, and Rural* (ed: B. Jan McCulloch) The Haworth Press, Inc., 1998, pp. 41-65. Single or multiple copies of this article are available for a fee from The Haworth Document Delivery Service [1-800-342-9678, 9:00 a.m. - 5:00 p.m. (EST). E-mail address: getinfo@haworthpressinc.com].

The economic position of older women in rural or nonmetropolitan areas of the United States is worse than that of their counterparts in urban or metropolitan areas (Coward, 1987; Glasgow, 1988; McLaughlin & Holden, 1993). This differential has been documented by cross-sectional studies, and in studies using panel data that examine how women's economic status changes as they age. Nonmetro women have been found to have higher risks of becoming poor and lower risks of leaving poverty as they grow older (McLaughlin & Jensen, 1995; Jensen & McLaughlin, 1997). Older rural women not only have lower incomes overall, they also spend more years in poverty than older urban women.

What is missing from many of these prior studies is the ability to determine whether the position of nonmetro relative to metro older women is improving or worsening over time. This paper addresses whether more recent cohorts of older nonmetro women are doing better economically than earlier cohorts, and whether the gap in income and poverty between metropolitan and nonmetropolitan women has narrowed among more recent cohorts. Data from the 1970, 1980, and 1990 Public Use Microdata samples of the U.S. Bureau of the Census are used to compare the household incomes of older metro and nonmetro women from different birth cohorts as they age.

FACTORS THAT INFLUENCE OLDER WOMEN'S ECONOMIC WELL-BEING

Prior research has documented declines in poverty among older Americans over the past few decades and increases in the incomes of elders relative to those of persons in other age groups (Duncan & Smith, 1989; Ross, Danziger & Smolensky, 1987). For example, the poverty rate among persons 65 and over was 24.6% in 1970 and dropped to 12.2% in 1987 (Smeeding, 1990). An increase in the inequality of income among America's elders has also been documented (Crystal & Shea, 1990; Crystal & Waehrer, 1996). Thus, while average incomes have increased and poverty rates dropped, there is strong evidence that the variability in economic well-being within the elderly population has increased (Crystal & Shea, 1990), and increases with age within a cohort of elders (Crystal & Waehrer, 1996). This raises two questions; first, what are the explanations for the improvement in elders' economic well-being, and second, what are the factors that are associated with elders locating in the high or low end of the income distribution?

Cohort succession provides one explanation for the improvement in the economic well-being of elders. Cohorts now entering older ages are economically better-off than earlier cohorts, so as individuals in the older cohorts die, they are replaced by wealthier, younger cohorts (Duncan, Hill, & Rodgers, 1986; Riley, 1973; Ross, Danziger & Smolensky, 1987). Higher mortality of low SES individuals within each cohort also makes it appear as though the economic well-being of a cohort improves with age. Those with lower socio-economic status tend to die at younger ages, so survivors in a cohort tend to be wealthier individuals. An alternative explanation is that the incomes of individual elders actually increase as they age.

Understanding the distribution of incomes among elders requires identify-ing those characteristics of individuals and their life experiences that influ-ence household income. Prior studies of elders' economic well-being and poverty have provided strong evidence of the factors that are most often related to lower incomes and higher probability of being or becoming poor (Burkhauser, Holden & Feaster, 1988; Coe, 1988; Henretta & Campbell, 1976; Holden, Burkhauser & Feaster, 1988; Holden, Burkhauser & Myers, 1986). These factors include education, labor force status, marital status and living arrangements, race and residence (Glasgow, 1988; Hardy & Hazelrigg, 1993). These characteristics are important for both men and women, and they also have been found to be critical in understanding differences in economic well-being among metro and nonmetro elders (Glasgow, 1988; McLaughlin & Jensen, 1993; 1995; Kivett & Schwenk, 1994; Lee & Lassey, 1980). Differ-ences in the composition of the nonmetro and metro elderly population do influence poverty risks. The importance of these compositional characteris-tics for women's economic well-being at older ages will be briefly described, and then important differences that influence the metro and nonmetro gap in older women's income and poverty are discussed. Then, the variation of these factors by birth cohort is described, providing insight into the process by which elderly women's incomes vary across cohorts.

Education, a major indicator of human capital and social stratification, is linked to incomes and poverty in old age through opportunities for high paying jobs and jobs with benefits, as well as through better health. In addi-tion, more highly educated individuals may be better able to plan for retire-ment. Henretta and Campbell (1976) discuss status maintenance into old age; Crystal and Shea (1990) propose that differences in economic well-being are exaggerated in old age through cumulative advantages and cumulative disad-vantages, while O'Rand (1996) builds on this notion. Essentially, those who do well as adults continue to do well, or even better, in old age on a variety of indicators of well-being. Since many women obtain a large share of house-hold income from their spouse, the link between women's own education and household income can be weakened, unless husbands and wives have similar educational levels. Alternatively, better educated widows or divorced or sep-arated women may be better able to manage and organize the resources they have in planning for old age.

Nonmetropolitan women's educational attainment has lagged behind that of metropolitan women, placing them at a disadvantage in the labor market.

Similarly, the educational attainment of nonmetropolitan men is lower than that of metropolitan men (McLaughlin & Jensen, 1998; Glasgow, Holden, McLaughlin & Rowles, 1993). This lower educational attainment limits employment options and the more restricted labor market opportunities in nonmetropolitan areas result in lower returns to education in nonmetro than in metro labor markets for both men and women (McLaughlin & Perman, 1991), increasing the risk of low income and poverty in old age.

Women's current labor force participation has a direct effect on income since employment generates earnings. Women who remain in the labor force rather than retire tend to have higher household incomes than those who have exited or never entered the labor force (Crystal & Waehrer, 1996; Hardy & Hazelrigg, 1993). Prior labor force experience also influences women's household income. Many older women had limited or interrupted labor force experience because of gender role conflicts over the life course (Hatch, 1990; Pienta, Burr & Mutchler, 1994). Nonmetropolitan women's lower levels of labor force participation, and their greater likelihood of having worked on family farms without pay or earnings records, places them at a distinct disadvantage in qualifying for Social Security or pension benefits based on their own employment histories (Bokemeier, Sachs, & Keith, 1983; Burkhauser & Duncan, 1989; Hatch, 1990; Ozawa, 1995; Smith & Moen, 1988). Women who participated in the labor force were often funneled into highly sex-segregated occupations dampening the benefits of higher educational attainment (Hardy & Hazelrigg, 1993; Reskin & Hartmann, 1986). In addition, women were less likely to have enough years of employment to be vested in pensions, and to be employed in industries or occupations with pension coverage (Beller, 1981; Quadagno, 1988). In 1987, 32% of men and 13.6% of women received a pension under the private retirement system (Olson, 1994). These percentages are likely to be lower in nonmetro areas. Women's lower earnings when they are in the labor force place them at a further disadvantage in terms of the benefit amounts they actually receive (Reskin & Hartmann, 1986).

Marital status is a primary determinant of older women's economic well-being. Married women have the highest incomes and the lowest poverty rates because of the contribution of husbands to household income (Ozawa, 1995). Never-married women tend to have adequate incomes, largely because these women, regardless of cohort, were employed (Ross, Danziger & Smolensky, 1987), and so had some access to pensions and Social Security (Choi, 1995; 1996; Reskin & Hartmann, 1986). Divorced and separated women have the lowest incomes, and the timing of divorce influences economic well-being (Choi, 1995; Morgan, 1991). Divorced women may lose access to important employment-related resources that have accrued to their spouses (Holden & Smock, 1991; Morgan, 1991; Warlick, 1985), such as current earnings, pension benefits, a full share of Social Security, and other assets accumulated during the marriage (Burkhauser & Duncan, 1991; Morgan, 1991; Olson, 1994).

Widowed women have lower incomes than married couples and women are much more likely to become widowed than men. In 1990, 82.3% of nonmetro women ages 85 and over were widowed, compared with 40% of this cohort being widowed in 1970 at ages 65 to 74 (data not shown). Widows often experience drops in income coincident with their spouses' deaths (Burkhauser, Butler & Holden, 1991), due to loss of the spouse's earnings, pension benefits, and as a result of changes in Social Security benefits triggered by the death of the spouse (Bound, Duncan, Laren, & Oleinick, 1991; Zick & Smith, 1986; 1991). Many women are reliant on a spouse's pension income. If a woman's spouse selected a sole survivor option, those pension benefits end with the death of the spouse. Even a joint-survivor option can drastically cut the pension benefit on the death of the covered spouse (to 50% of the full benefit). Societal preferences that discouraged women from working outside the home and discrimination against women in the workplace have affected women's access to Social Security and pension benefits.

Nonmetropolitan women are especially disadvantaged because of their lower labor force participation, the more restricted job opportunities and lower wages available in nonmetro areas, and the tendency for firms to be smaller and thus less likely to offer pension benefits (Clark, Ghent & Headen, 1994; Lonsdale & Seylor, 1979; Tickamyer & Bokemeier, 1988; Tickamyer & Duncan, 1990). As indicated above, nonmetro women have diminished access to these benefits not only because of their own situation, but because their spouses also face the same restricted opportunity labor markets. Prior research has documented the lower levels of Social Security and pension benefits paid to nonmetro residents (McLaughlin & Holden, 1993), and it has shown that nonmetro poor and nonpoor are less likely to receive interest and dividends income than metro individuals (McLaughlin & Jensen, 1993) suggesting a lessened ability to save towards retirement.

Race is another important correlate of income among older women. Minorities have lower incomes and higher poverty rates than white women at all ages, and across marital statuses. This occurs despite African American women's greater labor force participation (Ozawa, 1995). Racial and gender segregation combine to place minority women at the very bottom in access to good occupations and earnings. Ozawa (1995) documents that the low wages paid to African American women often prevent all quarters of employment being counted towards determination of Social Security benefits. Domestic service work only came under Social Security coverage in 1950. Among the beneficiaries that Ozawa studied, 54% of African American women were employed in service occupations as their longest job, compared to 14% of white and 25% of Hispanic women. Hispanic women had lower attachment to the labor force throughout their lives and are disadvantaged in that regard.

Minorities in nonmetropolitan areas face especially difficult labor market conditions (Jensen & Tienda, 1989). Most African Americans in nonmetro areas reside in the South, a region that has historically been associated with the poorest educational and labor market opportunities for minorities (Fossett & Seibert, 1997; Falk, Talley, & Rank, 1993), and that has failed to invest in areas with high concentrations of minority populations (Colclough, 1988). The poverty rate in 1990 among Blacks ages 65 and over was higher in nonmetro areas (41.5%) than in the central cities of metropolitan areas (27.9%). Elderly Hispanics also had slightly higher poverty rates in nonmetro areas than in central cities in 1990 (McLaughlin & Jensen, 1993).

Most of the factors that place older women at greater risk of poverty and that result in lower incomes are exacerbated in nonmetropolitan areas. Women in nonmetropolitan areas, especially those in earlier cohorts, have lower levels of educational attainment, they are less likely to have any labor force experience, and race is especially detrimental to economic well-being in nonmetro areas. Even though women in nonmetro areas are more likely to have remained married, the benefits of marriage are not as great because job opportunities for their spouses were fewer and lower quality. Men in nonmetropolitan areas have lower earnings and lower educational levels than metro men, and jobs in nonmetro areas are less likely to be in large firms or to be covered by unions, and thus are limited in pension coverage and other benefits. These differences support the importance of considering women's characteristics when comparing incomes among metro and nonmetro women. Differential returns to human capital in nonmetro and metro areas (McLaughlin & Perman, 1991) further suggest that the metro/nonmetro difference in incomes will remain after the compositional differences are controlled, and that it is essential to examine whether characteristics that affect older women's incomes differ in metro and nonmetro areas.

Why Is a Cohort Analysis Useful?

Most studies compare women of different ages simultaneously, or they follow a single birth cohort of women over time. Neither approach provides a clear indication of whether the economic situation of older women is improving because of the movement of younger, wealthier cohorts into older ages or because of increases in income within cohorts as women age, or some combination of both. Cross-sectional studies often document the poorer economic positions of older women. But they cannot uncover the reasons older women do worse than younger women. Panel studies of a single birth cohort can show how older women's incomes change as they age, but they rarely contain individuals in several cohorts.

Prior studies that have examined cohort differences in income and poverty have focused on men or never-married women (Ross, Danziger & Smolensky, 1987). They find that more recent cohorts enter retirement age with more resources than the cohort before, and that average incomes decline with retirement, but then there is a slight gain in income at older ages. Women, however, remain economically vulnerable as they age (Duncan & Smith, 1989). Panel studies that have examined a single cohort of women find that women, especially widows, are more likely to experience decreases in income as they age.

Examining changes in income status both across and within cohorts requires that other factors that might change across cohorts (e.g., labor force participation, education) as well as those that change as individuals age (e.g., marital status, labor force participation) be considered. Factors that would result in cohort differences in economic well-being are described next.

The relationship between a woman's own education and her economic status should be stronger in more recent cohorts. This occurs largely through the greater labor force participation of women in younger cohorts that results from increases in women's educational attainment, likelihood of working, and earnings potential. Reductions in discrimination against women in the labor market should result in education having a stronger influence on the income of recent rather than earlier cohorts of older women, because women's earnings should more accurately reflect their human capital. Current labor force participation will increase women's income and lower their risks of poverty. The size of this effect will increase in more recent cohorts if greater sex segregation and discrimination against women in the earlier cohorts keeps those women's earnings lower than those of more recent cohorts, even after adjusting for inflation.

It is difficult to predict how marital status and living arrangements will affect older women's incomes across cohorts. Divorced or separated women in earlier cohorts will be worse off than divorced or separated women in the more recent cohorts. Yet more women in the younger cohorts are likely to be divorced or separated, or to have multiple marriages. Some of the changes in Social Security and pension benefits, and changes in divorce laws, offer some protection to women in more recent cohorts (Morgan, 1991; Holden & Smock, 1991). Women who become widowed also have better access to deceased spouses' pension benefits in more recent cohorts. Recent improvements in life expectancy also suggest that more recent cohorts will become widowed at later ages than women in earlier cohorts, delaying the onset of economic decline. At the same time as the situation for divorced and separated or widowed women may have improved in more recent cohorts, the situation of married women has improved. As more women entered the labor force, the incomes of dual-income married couples outpaced those of single-earner married couples (Cancian, Danziger & Gottschalk, 1994), improving the ability of these couples to accumulate assets towards retirement. Thus, the overall effect of marital status is difficult to predict.

Racial differences in older women's income should have declined in more recent cohorts. The decline in racial discrimination and segregation over the past three decades should contribute to a decline in racial differences in women's household income.

Nonmetropolitan women have become more like metropolitan women in more recent cohorts in terms of their labor force participation and educational attainment, leading to an expectation that the gap in income and poverty between metro and nonmetro older women would decrease. Despite this narrowing of demographic characteristics, the types and quality of jobs available in nonmetro compared to metro areas remain more limited, making an overall prediction of closure of the metro/nonmetro gap in older women's income difficult.

In this study, a cohort analysis is conducted to discern the relative economic positions of older metro and nonmetro women. The income and poverty gap between women in these areas is assessed to determine if they have been growing or declining in recent cohorts, whether the gap declines when differences in characteristics of the women are controlled, and whether particular factors are more or less important across cohorts for determining older women's incomes.

DATA AND METHODS

A cohort analysis requires the use of a data source that (1) provides information on women from several birth cohorts at the same age, (2) includes enough women to allow a comparison of metropolitan and nonmetropolitan women, and (3) offers enough consistency in measures over time for reliable analyses to be conducted. The only data that meet these three criteria are the Public Use Samples of the U.S. Census of Population and Housing. By combining data from the 1970, 1980 and 1990 Censuses of Population and Housing, it is possible to examine four different birth cohorts (See Table 1). Institutionalized women are not included in the sample used in this study.

The first step in the cohort analysis is to examine women's household income by age group, year, and birth cohort for metro and nonmetro women. This gives an initial assessment of whether metro and nonmetro women's economic status has improved or declined within and across cohorts. Multivariate models of women's income by birth cohort are then estimated to determine whether nonmetro women remain disadvantaged with composition controlled, and if that disadvantage is increasing or declining. A final assess-

TABLE 1. Cohorts Used in This Study

	1970	1980	1990
Birth Cohort 1 Born 1896-1905	65 to 74 years	75 to 84 years	85 years and older
Birth Cohort 2 Born 1906-1915	55 to 64 years	65 to 74 years	75 to 84 years
Birth Cohort 3 Born 1916-1925	- - -	55 to 64 years	65 to 74 years
Birth Cohort 4 Born 1926-1935	- - -	- - -	55 to 64 years

ment examines whether the factors that influence older women's economic well-being differ for metro and nonmetro women within cohorts.

Measures

Measures used in this analysis are straightforward. Only those measures that require additional explanation are discussed here. The dependent variable in the analysis is the household income for the household in which these older women lived. A problem encountered in the use of the household income data is the change in the top income category across Census years. In 1970, incomes above $50,000 were coded as $50,000, in 1979 the top income category was $75,000, and in 1989 it was $999,999. To improve consistency in measures across census years, the 1969 and 1979 incomes were inflated to 1989 dollars using the Consumer Price Index, and then a top category of $128,000 was applied to all years. This value was the minimum inflation-adjusted top income category across the three census years. Mean household incomes in 1989 dollars are reported, but poverty rates and median income values provide the best indicators for comparisons of economic well-being across cohorts and census years because they are not influenced by the top income category.

Changes in definitions of race and ethnicity, and willingness to report ethnicity have varied across Census years. In each year, the available information on race and Hispanic ethnicity was used to create categories that were as consistent as possible. The most change occurred in the treatment of Spanish descent and Hispanic ethnicity.

Another difficulty in describing older women's economic status is the link between living arrangements and marital status. In the multivariate analysis, it was necessary to combine marital status and living arrangements into a single set of dummy variables. These categories are married; divorced or separated and living alone; never married and living alone; widowed and living alone; with the final category women who were divorced or separated, never married or widowed and not living alone. The women in this last category are living with other unrelated adults, or in households with their own children or other relatives.

A final difficulty in comparing older women by birth cohort across Census years from 1970 to 1990 using the Public Use Microdata Samples is the inability to adjust for the changing classification of counties as metropolitan. Only 116 counties that were nonmetropolitan in 1970 had become metropolitan by 1990. These counties contained only 6.4% of elders suggesting that the reclassification has minimal influence on residential comparisons of elders (McLaughlin and Jensen 1998).

RESULTS

The economic position of older women in the United States by birth cohort and year (or age) is shown in Table 2. Mean and median household income, and the percentage of women in poor households are reported. Looking across a row in the table, it is possible to observe the change in household income or poverty status as the cohort ages. For example, the first birth cohort (born 1896 to 1905) was ages 65 to 74 years in 1970, ages 75 to 84 in 1980, and ages 85 and over in 1990 (there is no adjustment for mortality in the cohort between census years).[1]

Rather than concentrate on the overall figures in Table 2, Table 3 which shows the mean and median household incomes and poverty rates by birth cohort and year for nonmetro and metro women is discussed in detail. The mean household income of nonmetro women drops as the first birth cohort ages from 65 to 74 to 75 to 84 years of age (from $17,429 to $16,290). There is a very slight rise in mean household income from 1980 to 1990 as these women age into their late 80s and early 90s (from $16,290 to $16,555). While the mean values are reported, the medians provide a better measure for comparison. Looking at median household income for the nonmetro women in cohort 1, the median income drops from $10,474 in 1970 when the women were 65 to 74, to $10,265 when the women were ages 75 to 84 in 1980, and then drops again to $9,797 in 1990. This is different from the pattern for metro women, where not only are median incomes much higher in each year, there is a rise in median income from 1980 to 1990 as the first cohort ages to be 85 and over. This rise may reflect the greater longevity of those with higher economic status, and is consistent with earlier studies (Ross, Danziger, &

TABLE 2. Descriptive Statistics on Household Income and Poverty Prevalence for Women by Birth Cohort and Year (CPI adjusted to 1989 dollars)

	Panel A. Mean Household Income (standard deviation in parentheses)		
	1970	1980	1990
Birth Cohort 1 Born 1896-1905	$22,777 (25,565)	$20,731 (21,907)	$22,045 (23,756)
Birth Cohort 2 Born 1906-1915	33,409 (28,147)	23,662 (22,034)	21,908 (22,531)
Birth Cohort 3 Born 1916-1925	- - -	35,015 (26,833)	27,180 (23,989)
Birth Cohort 4 Born 1926-1935	- - -	- - -	37,731 (28,969)
	Panel B. Median Household Income		
Birth Cohort 1	$13,853	$12,537	$12,801
Birth Cohort 2	26,692	16,721	13,900
Birth Cohort 3	- - -	28,797	20,109
Birth Cohort 4	- - -	- - -	30,420
	Panel C. Percentage of Women in Poor Households		
Birth Cohort 1	27.2	20.6	22.3
Birth Cohort 2	14.8	15.1	19.1
Birth Cohort 3	- - -	11.1	12.8
Birth Cohort 4	- - -	- - -	10.5

*The 1990 census reported incomes up to $999,999. while the 1980 census topcoded income at $75,000, and the 1970 census at $50,000. To insure that the change in topcoding of income across years does not bias the comparisons all incomes were adjusted to 1989 dollars using the Consumer Price Index and then a top code of $128,000 was applied to all years. The value $128,000 was selected because it is the lower CPI adjusted top code (the value for the 1980 census).

Smolensky, 1987), but the improvement is not apparent among nonmetro women.

Poverty rates for nonmetro women show a high of 36.4 percent for cohort 1 at ages 65 to 74, that drops to 29 percent in 1980 and rises slightly to 30.8 percent in 1990 (ages 85 and over). For metro women, poverty rates show the same pattern, but poverty rates are much lower than those for nonmetro women. The metro pattern suggests that incomes are becoming less equal as this cohort ages, consistent with the findings of Crystal and Waehrer (1996).

TABLE 3. Descriptive Statistics on Household Income and Poverty Prevalence for Women by Birth Cohort and Year

	Panel A. Mean Household Income (standard deviation in parentheses)					
	Metropolitan			Nonmetropolitan		
	1970	1980	1990	1970	1980	1990
Birth Cohort 1 Born 1896-1905	25,978 (27,010)	22,508 (23,161)	24,778 (25,682)	17,429 (21,491)	16,290 (17,640)	16,555 (18,114)
Birth Cohort 2 Born 1906-1915	36,693 (28,768)	25,445 (23,186)	24,466 (4,403)	26,540 (25,483)	19,251 (18,149)	16,748 (17,042)
Birth Cohort 3 Born 1916-1925	- - -	37,490 (27,652)	29,895 (25,551)	- - -	28,184 (23,094)	21,190 (18,782)
Birth Cohort 4 Born 1926-1935	- - -	- - -	41,391 (30,384)	- - -	- - -	29,166 (23,216)
	Panel B. Median Household Income					
	Metropolitan			Nonmetropolitan		
Birth Cohort 1	16,218	13,698	14,987	10,474	10,265	9,797
Birth Cohort 2	30,070	18,130	15,768	19,934	13,749	10,983
Birth Cohort 3	- - -	31,359	22,460	- - -	22,319	15,956
Birth Cohort 4	- - -	- - -	34,058	- - -	- - -	23,660
	Panel C. Percentage of Women in Poor Households					
	Metropolitan			Nonmetropolitan		
Birth Cohort 1	22.4	17.3	18.1	36.4	29.0	30.8
Birth Cohort 2	11.4	12.7	15.6	22.2	20.9	26.1
Birth Cohort 3	- - -	9.7	10.8	- - -	15.2	17.4
Birth Cohort 4	- - -	- - -	9.0	- - -	- - -	14.1

*Household incomes are adjusted to 1989 dollars using the Consumer Price Index and each year is top coded at $128,000.

The nonmetro patterns are ambiguous as to whether income inequality increases as the cohort ages.

The cohort of women born between 1906 and 1915 shows a steady decline in income from ages 55 to 64 through ages 75 to 84. The pattern was consistent for nonmetro and metro women. Income information for this cohort at ages 85 and over is not yet available to determine whether or not their incomes will increase at that age. From 1970 to 1980, nonmetro poverty rates declined in cohort 2 (from 22.2 to 20.9), with an increase to 26.1 percent in 1990. Metro poverty rates increased in each year as cohort 2 aged. The nonmetro and metro women born from 1916 to 1925 show a sharp decline in mean and median income and increases in poverty prevalence from ages 55 to 64 to ages 65 to 74. Overall, these findings suggest that as a birth cohort of women ages, their median household income tends to drop. The drop in poverty for birth cohort 1 from 1970 to 1980 is consistent with Social Security benefit increases put in place in the late 1960s and early 1970s (Gendell & Siegel, 1996), the establishment of the annual cost-of-living increase in 1972, and the implementation of the Supplemental Security Income program in 1974 (Ozawa, 1995). It also is consistent with higher mortality among those with lower socioeconomic status, reducing the poor in the cohort.

The question of whether more recent cohorts of women are better off economically at a given age than earlier cohorts requires comparing incomes and poverty rates along the diagonals (down and to the right) of Table 3. Again looking at nonmetro women, women in birth cohort 1 (born between 1896 and 1905) had a median household income of $10,474 when they were 65 to 74 years old in 1970. The second birth cohort was ages 65 to 74 in 1980, and had a median household income of $13,749. The third birth cohort (born 1916 to 1925) reported a median household income of $15,956 at ages 65 to 74 (in 1990). These show a steady increase in median household incomes across cohorts. Poverty rates for women ages 65 to 74 across these three birth cohorts decreased from 36.4 percent to 17.4 percent, from the oldest to the youngest cohort, respectively. In both comparisons, nonmetro women's economic status has improved in more recent cohorts. The same pattern holds for metro women, but again the median incomes are substantially higher and the poverty rates much lower than those for nonmetro women.

Among older women ages 55 to 64 there is a similar pattern of increasing median household incomes by birth cohort. Median income at ages 55 to 64 (in 1970) for the second birth cohort of nonmetro women was $19,934, which by the time the fourth birth cohort was 55 to 64 years of age in 1990, had increased to $23,660. Poverty rates had declined from 22.2 percent for the second birth cohort in 1970 to 14.1 percent for the fourth in 1990. This shows improvement from oldest to youngest cohorts in economic well-being for nonmetro women ages 55 to 64 across three birth cohorts. The same pattern holds for metro women, but incomes are higher and poverty rates lower.

Among those ages 75 to 84, only two birth cohorts can be compared with the data available. This comparison, for the first and second birth cohorts in 1980 and 1990, shows an increase in nonmetro women's median household income from $10,265 to $10,983, and an almost three percent drop in poverty prevalence (29.0 to 26.1). These comparisons provide clear evidence that the economic well-being of more recent cohorts is higher than that of older cohorts of women at the same age.

Equally important in Table 3 is the much lower mean and median household incomes of nonmetropolitan older women, and their higher poverty rates. Median incomes of nonmetro women ranged from 64.6 to 75.6 percent of the household incomes of metro women in the same age and birth cohort (numbers not shown). Nonmetro women's household incomes were strongest relative to metro women in the 1980 data. By 1990, however, the ratios had dropped so that nonmetro older women had median incomes roughly 70% of those reported by metro women. Thus, in these descriptive statistics there is evidence of a closing of the metro/nonmetro gap in median earnings from 1970 to 1980, but it widens again from 1980 to 1990.

Multivariate Models of Older Women's Household Income

The metro/nonmetro differences in income levels and the quite different experiences of women from different birth cohorts suggest that women's characteristics may play a large role in determining differences in household income. To test whether nonmetro incomes remain lower when differences in education, marital status and living arrangements, race and age are controlled, ordinary least squares regression models of household income for women in each birth cohort were estimated separately. This involved pooling the information for women in a particular birth cohort across Census years.

The first model in Table 4 shows the estimated regression coefficients for women born from 1896 to 1905. After controlling for compositional differences, nonmetro women still had incomes $6,158 less than those of metro women. But, adding these controls resulted in a modest reduction in the nonmetro coefficient, when compared with a model that contained only nonmetro as the independent variable (coefficient = $7,355, not shown).

In the model for the second birth cohort, nonmetro residence reduces incomes by $7,481 when other factors are controlled, a statistically significant increase in the negative influence of nonmetro residence over that in the first birth cohort. As expected, the influence of education increased, as did the effect of being married. Being divorced and living alone became more detrimental to household income from the first to the second cohort, as did the influence of living in the South, being Hispanic and ages 75 to 84. The advantage of being unmarried and living with others declined from the first to the second cohort.

The third model shows the results for the third birth cohort, women born from 1916 to 1925. The negative influence of nonmetro residence for the second birth cohort was not statistically different from that for the third birth cohort ($-7,481$ and $-7,584$, respectively), and there is a continued increase in the influence of education and being married for women's house-

TABLE 4. Ordinary Least Squares Regression of Women's Characteristics on Household Income by Birth Cohort (data are from the 1970, 1980 and 1990 Censuses of Population and Housing)

	Birth Cohort 1 (1896 to 1905)	Birth Cohort 2 (1906 to 1915)	Birth Cohort 3 (1916 to 1925)	Birth Cohort 4 (1926 to 1935)
Intercept	16,694***	21,053***a	20,860***	19,710***c
Nonmetropolitan	− 6,158***	− 7,481***a	− 7,584***	− 11,113***c
High school	5,718***	6,781***a	7,890***b	9,216***c
> High school	11,360***	16,535***a	20,483***b	25,823***c
Married	15,056***	18,759***a	21,178***b	25,753***c
Divorce and alone	− 734*	− 1,806***a	− 2,753***b	− 2,982***
Never married and alone	− 183	− 479	− 521	− 1,437*
Unmarried and not alone	23,677***	20,533***a	18,560***b	16,975***c
Fertility (children ever born)	− 57*	15a	156***b	198
South	− 1,733***	− 2,473***a	− 2,010***b	− 3,784***c
Black	− 10,721***	− 10,511***	− 10,371***	− 9,352***
White	− 3,047***	2,795***	− 3,278***	− 2,868***
Hispanic	− 2,320***	− 4,121***a	− 4,384***	− 4,532***
Out of the labor force	− 5,322***	− 5,621***	− 6,677***b	− 7,936***c
age 65 to 74	——	− 3,278***	− 2,178***b	——
age 75 to 84	2,163***	− 1,651***a	——	——
age 85 and over	3,939***	——	——	——
R²	0.251	0.265	0.271	0.276
Sample size	130,178	248,012	226,634	125,744

*p ≤.05; **p ≤.01; ***p ≤.001
a Coefficeints statistically different for birth cohorts 1 and 2
bCoefficients statistically different for birth cohorts 2 and 3
cCoefficients statistically different for birth cohorts 3 and 4

hold income. Being divorced or separated, compared to being widowed and living alone, was more detrimental for the third than the second birth cohort. Being unmarried and living alone became less protective from the second to the third birth cohort. Racial and ethnic differentials in incomes did not change significantly from the second to the third birth cohort. Being age 65 to 74, compared to 55 to 64, results in a decline in household income that diminishes from the second to the third cohort. The cost of being out of the labor force increased, however.

The final model in Table 4 shows the women's household income model for women born between 1926 and 1935, who were ages 55 to 64 in 1990. Nonmetro women have incomes $11,113 less than metro women, even with other factors controlled. The influence of education once again has increased, possibly showing the tighter link between women's own education and their household income, as well as indicating better returns for women's work in the labor market. The effect of being married increases when compared with the earlier cohorts, while the influences of being divorced or separated and never married and living alone have not changed. While still very protective, the benefits for unmarried women of living with someone else continued to decline. The racial differentials do not change. The costs of being out of the labor force increase from the third to the fourth cohort.

One question these analyses raise is whether the influence of nonmetro residence differs, not only by birth cohort, but by age of the women in each cohort (e.g., the nonmetro effect is so large in the fourth birth cohort because only women ages 55 to 64 were part of this cohort). To test whether this is the case, household income models for each birth cohort similar to those in Table 4 were estimated, but age group by nonmetro residence interactions were added. The difference for each age group and birth cohort in the influence of nonmetro residence is shown in Table 5. The numbers in the table are the metro values minus the nonmetro values that result from combining the nonmetro by age group interactions with the main effects for nonmetro residence and age group.

The patterns in the table are not clear-cut. The gap in the nonmetro and

TABLE 5. Difference in Metro and Nonmetro Effects on Household Income by Age Group and Birth Cohort (based on interaction terms and main effects from OLS regressions models estimated by birth cohort)

	Metro Effect Minus Nonmetro Effect		
	1970	1980	1990
Birth Cohort 1	7,159 (ages 65 to 74)	6,053 (ages 75 to 84)	8,988 (ages 85+)
Birth Cohort 2	- - 10,219 (age 55 to 64)	467 (ages 65 to 74)	3,006 (ages 75 to 84)
Birth Cohort 3	- - -	- - 7,958 (age 55 to 64)	4,833 (ages 65 to 74)
Birth Cohort 4			11,113 (ages 55 to 64)

metro effect diminishes as women in birth cohort 1 age from 65 to 74 to 75 to 84 (from $7,159 to $6,053), and as women in birth cohorts 2 and 3 age from 55 to 64 to 65 to 74 ($10,219 to $467 and $7,590 to $4,833). The gap increases again for women in birth cohort 1 as they age from 75 to 84 to 85 and over, and for women in birth cohort 2 as they age from 65 to 74 to 75 to 84 (from $467 to $3,006). If women of the same age in different cohorts are compared, a decline in the metro-nonmetro gap in household income is observed from 1970 to 1980 regardless of age.

The gap swings upward from 1980 to 1990, with one exception. The metro-nonmetro gap declines for women ages 75 to 84 in birth cohort 1 and birth cohort 2 from 1980 to 1990, from $6,053 to $3,006. These persistent gaps in metro-nonmetro income are especially important since they control for differences across cohorts and age groups in marital status, education, labor force participation and race.

The final step in the empirical analysis is to determine whether factors that influence older women's household income differ for women in metro and nonmetro areas. These differences could help explain the metro-nonmetro gap in household income. Table 6 shows results of models estimated separately by residence for each of the first three birth cohorts. Statistically different coefficients in the metro and nonmetro models for the same birth cohort are indicated by an a ([a]).

Most notably, for every cohort, the effects of the intercept, high school education, more than high school, being married, and unmarried and living with others are greater for metro than nonmetro women. Nonmetro women pay a higher price for fertility. Each additional child decreases nonmetro women's household income in old age at least $80 across cohorts, while fertility increases metro women's incomes in the second and third birth cohorts.

Residence in the South is more detrimental for metro women in the second and third birth cohorts; the effect is the same for metro and nonmetro women in the first birth cohort. This suggests interesting changes in the South over these decades, both in terms of economic development, but also retirement in-migration.

In each birth cohort, being Black or Hispanic had a significantly larger negative effect on income in metropolitan than nonmetroplitan areas, as did being White (compared to other race women). Being out of the labor force diminished household incomes more in nonmetro than metro households for birth cohort 2, but in birth cohort 3 the reverse was true. Equally important in these models of household income is the consistently significantly lower intercept in every nonmetro model, compared to the metro model for the same birth cohort. Thus, the intercept establishes a lower base household income for nonmetro than metro older women.

Overall, these models estimated separately for metro and nonmetro

TABLE 6. Ordinary Least Squares Regression of Women's Characteristics on Household Income by Birth Cohort and Residence (data are from the 1970, 1980 and 1990 Censuses of Population and Housing)

	Birth Cohort 1 (1896-1905)		Birth Cohort 2 (1906-1925)		Birth Cohort 3 (1916-1925)	
	Metropolitan	Nonmetropolitan	Metropolitan	Nonmetropolitan	Metropolitan	Nonmetropolitan
Intercept	16,587	9,847[a]	20,806	12,164[a]	19,522	14,756[a]
High school	5,966	5,156[a]	6,988	6,271[a]	8,211	7,114[a]
> High school	11,971	10,058[a]	17,323	14,702[a]	21,293	17,919[a]
Married	17,053	10,961[a]	20,781	14,113[a]	23,158	16,003[a]
Divorced and alone	-266 (ns)	-602 (ns)	-1,310	-1,799	-2,332	-2,335
Never married & alone	268 (ns)	-456 (ns)	70 (ns)	-670 (ns)	377 (ns)	-1,641[a]
Unmarried & not alone	25,995	17,958[a]	22,621	15,125[a]	20,187	14,074[a]
Fertility	-3 (ns)	-153[a]	76	-98[a]	240	-83[a]
South	-1,670	-1,850	-2,696	-2,090	-2,492	-1,410[a]
Black	-12,252	-5,355[a]	-11,991	-4,565[a]	-11,125	-5,448[a]
White	-3,894	516 (ns)[a]	-3,755	1,487[a]	-3,699	-175 (ns)[a]
Hispanic	-2,968	-432 (ns)[a]	-4,722	-1,622[a]	-4,661	-2,370[a]
Out of labor force	-5,448	-4,897	-5,319	-6,014[a]	-7,028	-5,610[a]
age 65 to 74	—	—	-4,643	-518[a]	-2,036	-2,670[a]
age 75 to 84	1,633	-3,215[a]	-2,500	-95 (ns)[a]	—	—
age 85 and over	3,821	4,024	—	—	—	—
R2	0.243	0.223	0.260	0.230	0.263	0.236
Sample size	88,564	41,615	170,392	77,621	161,129	65,506

[a]The metro and nonmetro coefficients are statistically different in the cohort. ns indicates that the coefficient is not statistically different from zero.

58

women by birth cohort reveal a great deal of change in the factors that differ by residence in influencing women's household incomes. Clearly, marital status is a key determinant of older women's economic well-being, and as expected, metro women benefit much more from being married or living in a household with others. Both of these effects are tied to the presence of a male earner, either the spouse or another adult male. These larger effects in metro areas support the argument that nonmetro men are particularly disadvantaged while they are in the labor force, and then again when they exit the labor force with less accumulated assets, lower access to pensions, and lower benefit levels of Social Security and pensions. This translates into lower economic well-being for nonmetro women. The larger negative influence of fertility for nonmetro women further supports the idea that nonmetro households face more limited economic opportunities, and that the costs of raising additional children prevent nonmetro households from accumulating assets to use in retirement, and a larger number of children may be more likely to keep nonmetro than metro women from entering the labor force.

DISCUSSION AND CONCLUSIONS

The main purpose of this research was to determine whether nonmetro women born more recently are better-off economically than older cohorts of nonmetro women, and whether the economic position of nonmetro older women relative to metro older women has improved. There was clear evidence that the improvement in economic well-being among older women in recent years results from the increased household incomes that younger cohorts bring with them as they enter old age. There also was strong evidence of a decline in incomes as women within a cohort aged from 55 to 64 years of age to 65 to 74, the retirement years, with smaller declines as women aged to the 75 to 84 age group. There was mixed evidence for an increase in household income as a cohort aged from 75 to 84 to 85 and over.

Comparing metro and nonmetro older women, metro older women had higher household incomes than nonmetro older women even after controlling for differences in education, marital status, race and ethnicity, labor force participation and age. There also was an interesting pattern in the gap in metro and nonmetro older women's income that showed a decline in that income gap within cohorts from 1970 to 1980 and across cohorts for women of the same age from 1970 to 1980. This suggests an improvement in the relative position of nonmetro women. This improvement was short-lived, however, as comparisons within and across cohorts from 1980 to 1990 showed an increase in the metro-nonmetro income gap. Despite increases in older nonmetro women's incomes in more recent cohorts, the position of nonmetro women compared to metro women declined over the past decade.

This pattern of improvement and subsequent decline in nonmetro women's economic position relative to metro women is consistent with "period effect" explanations. The improvement in the economic conditions in nonmetro America is well-documented as is the relatively high in-migration to nonmetropolitan areas during the decade of the 1970s (Brown & Beale, 1981; Johnson, 1989). These trends would be consistent with improvement in economic well-being of nonmetro residents relative to metro residents. The 1980s were a time of economic retrenchment in nonmetro areas and slightly higher levels of out- than in-migration (Johnson, 1989; 1993), consistent with decline in nonmetro relative to metro incomes. It is relatively easy to argue that these economic factors explain the changing relative incomes of metro and nonmetro older women who are of working age, or whose husbands are of working age (those in the 55 to 64 age group). It is harder to explain why this pattern holds for women over age 65, who are unlikely to be in the labor force themselves, or to have a spouse in the labor market.

One explanation is that those who were 65 to 74 in 1990 were retiring or exiting the labor market during the decade of the 1980s. These individuals still may have been influenced by economic decline by being forced into early retirement, or by experiencing loss of pension benefits because of plant closure or failure of companies to pay promised benefits. Retirement patterns have changed in more recent cohorts. Those who retired during the 1960s and 1970s tended to make clean labor force exits, while those retiring during the 1980s were much more likely to have a transitional retirement period, where they left one job, but immediately took another in a phased exit from the labor force (Elder & Pavalko, 1993). To the extent that these new patterns of labor force exit and reentry are related to economic need, and economic conditions are worse in rural areas, then they could help explain the poorer position of 65 to 74 year olds in 1990. For women in these age groups, such trends in income could be affected by their own labor force experience, but it is more likely that they were influenced by the labor force experiences of the spouse.

Explaining the decline in relative position of nonmetro women ages 75 to 84 is more difficult. These individuals would have retired during the 1970s, a period of relative nonmetro prosperity. Once again, though, lower pension coverage, lower Social Security benefits, and more limited assets may result in a faster decline in income as nonmetro women age. Future research should examine the different types and amounts of income reported by older women across cohorts and age groups to begin to disentangle the relative importance of pensions, Social Security, and asset-based income. In the same vein, information about older women's own life-long labor force experiences, and those of their spouses, as well as changes in marital status could yield a significant increase in our ability to explain variation in older women's incomes.

Also important for understanding the economic well-being of future cohorts of elders are the changes observed in the influence of different characteristics on household income and the metro-nonmetro gap in income. The increasing importance of a woman's own education reflects more recent cohorts' greater labor force participation and accumulation of benefits in their own right. The increasing importance and positive effect on income of being married and of being unmarried but living with someone else suggests that a spouse's or other household member's income, and the sharing of income, is critically important for older women's economic well-being. The growing negative influence across cohorts of being divorced and living alone further indicates that women in this position face the worst economic circumstances, but there is no additional nonmetro disadvantage. This gap between older women with and without a spouse or other household member may explain a large part of the rising income inequality among elders. This disadvantage of being divorced or separated and living alone raises serious questions about the economic well-being of future cohorts of older women many more of whom have divorced or separated.

Such trends suggest that the gap between metro and nonmetro older women will continue to widen in the future. Both nonmetro men and women are disadvantaged relative to their metro counterparts in terms of earnings, pension coverage, and ability to accumulate assets towards retirement. As more women contribute to household incomes through labor force participation in both metro and nonmetro areas, the gap in married couples' incomes should increase. This will be especially true if nonmetro women's labor force participation continues to lag behind that of metro women. The lower pension coverage and lower earned Social Security benefits in nonmetro areas also will result in a continued gap in household income for widowed women, whether they rely on their own or a deceased spouse's benefits. An increase in the metro-nonmetro gap in future cohorts of older women is supported by the fact that the largest metro-nonmetro gap in household income occurred for women ages 55 to 64 in 1990, the youngest cohort examined.

Overall, it appears that changes in the relative incomes of metro and nonmetro older women are surprisingly tightly linked to recent economic conditions (growth or retrenchment) in their area of residence. Projections of the future economic well-being of older women, and the gap in incomes of metro and nonmetro older women, will continue to hinge on the marital status of older women, but it will be equally important to track the trends in economic conditions as future cohorts of elders enter their retirement years.

NOTE

1. One problem with using Census data to assess change in economic well-being of the cohort as it ages is that we do not have information on the individuals who have died between census years. The literature that links socioeconomic status and poverty to mortality risks describes a clear link between poverty and higher mortality risks at younger ages. Thus, those individuals who have died between the census years are more likely to have been poor or to have had lower incomes. Their deaths would have removed some poorer older women from the population, arguably resulting in an increase in mean or median incomes, if other factors did not change. In fact, Crystal and Waehrer (1996) conducted a cohort analysis of income inequality where they were able to include only survivors in one analysis and those who died between comparison points in another. They found that income inequality increased with the age of the cohort regardless of which group was used. This finding suggests that the results in this study would be similar if we were able to adjust for the deaths that occurred between census years.

REFERENCES

Beller, D.J. (1981). Coverage patterns of full-time employees under private retirement plans. *Social Security Bulletin*, *44*(7), 3-11, 47.

Bokemeier, J.L., Sachs, C., & Keith, V. (1983). Labor force participation of metropolitan, nonmetropolitan, and farm women: A comparative study. *Rural Sociology*, *48*, 515-539.

Bound, J., Duncan, G.J., Laren, D.S., & Oleinick, L. (1991). Poverty dynamics in widowhood. *Journal of Gerontology*, *46*, S115-S124.

Brown, D.L. & Beale, C.L. (1981). Diversity in post-1970 population trends. In A.H. Hawley & S.M. Mazie (eds.) *Nonmetropolitan America in Transition*. Chapel Hill, NC: The University of North Carolina Press.

Burkhauser, R.V., Butler, J.S., & Holden, K.C. (1991). How the death of a spouse affects economic well-being after retirement: A hazard model approach. *Social Science Quarterly*, *70*, 3-23.

Burkhauser, R.V. & Duncan, G.J. (1989). Economic risks of gender roles: Income loss and life events over the life course. *Social Science Quarterly*, *70*, 3-22.

Burkhauser, R.V. & Duncan, G.J. (1991). United States public policy and the elderly: The disproportionate risk to the well-being of women. *Journal of Population Economics*, *4*, 217-231.

Burkhauser, R.V., Holden, K.C. & Feaster, D.J. (1988). Incidence, timing and events associated with poverty: A dynamic view of poverty in retirement. *Journal of Gerontology: Social Sciences*, *43*, S46-S52.

Cancian, M., Danziger, S. & Gottschalk, P. (1994). Working wives and family income inequality among married couples. In S. Danziger and P. Gottschalk (eds.) *Uneven Tides: Rising Inequality in America* (pp. 195-221). New York: Russell Sage Foundation.

Choi, N.G. (1995). Long-term elderly widows and divorcees: Similarities and differences. *Journal of Women & Aging*, *7*, 69-92.

Choi, N.G. (1996). The never-married and divorced elderly: Comparison of economic and health status, social support, and living arrangement. *Journal of Gerontological Social Work, 26*(1/2), 3-25.

Clark, R.L., Ghent, L.S. & Headen, Jr., A.E. (1994). Retiree health insurance and pension coverage: Variations by firm characteristics. *Journal of Gerontology, 49,* S53-S61.

Coe, R.D. (1988). A longitudinal examination of poverty in the elderly years. *The Gerontologist, 28,* 540-544.

Colclough, G. (1988). Uneven development and racial composition in the deep South, 1970-1980. *Rural Sociology, 53,* 73-86.

Coward, R.T. (1987). Poverty and aging in rural America. *Human Services in the Rural Environment, 10,* 41-47.

Crystal, S. & Shea, D. (1990). Cumulative advantage, cumulative disadvantage, and inequality among elderly people. *The Gerontologist, 30,* 437-443.

Crystal, S. & Waehrer, K. (1996). Later-life economic inequality in longitudinal perspective. *Journal of Gerontology, 51B,* S307-S318.

Duncan, G.J., Hill, M.S. & Rodgers, W. (1986). *The changing status of the young and old.* Survey Research Center, University of Michigan.

Duncan, G.J., & Smith, K.R. (1989). The rising affluence of the elderly: How far, how fair, and how frail? *Annual Review of Sociology, 15,* 261-89.

Elder, G.H., & Pavalko, E.K. (1993). Work careers in men's later years: Transitions, trajectories, and historical change. *Journal of Gerontology: Social Sciences, 48,* S180-S191.

Falk, W.W., Talley, C.R. & Rankin, B.H. (1993). Life in the forgotten South: The black belt. In T.A. Lyson & W.W. Falk (Eds.) *Forgotten Places: Uneven Development in Rural America* (pp. 53-75). Lawrence, KS: University Press of Kansas.

Fossett, M.A. & Seibert, M.T. (1997). *Long time coming: Racial inequality in the nonmetropolitan south, 1940-1990.* Boulder, CO: Westview Press.

Gendell, M., & Siegel, J.S. (1996). Trends in retirement age in the United States, 1955-1993, by sex and race. *Journal of Gerontology: Social Sciences, 51B,* S132-S139.

Glasgow, N. (1988). *The nonmetro elderly: Economic and demographic status.* Washington, DC: U.S. Department of Agriculture, Economic Research Service.

Glasgow, N., Holden, K.C., McLaughlin, D.K., & Rowles, G.D. (1993). The rural elderly and poverty. In Rural Sociological Society Task Force on Rural Poverty (Eds.), *Persistent poverty in rural America.* (pp. 259-291). Boulder, Co: Westview Press.

Hatch, L.R. (1990). Effects of work and family on women's later-life resources. *Research on Aging, 12,* 311-338.

Hardy, M.A., & Hazelrigg, L.E. (1993). The gender of poverty in an aging population. *Research on Aging, 15,* 243-278.

Henretta, J.C. & Campbell, R.T. (1976). Status attainment and status maintenance: A study of stratification in old age. *American Sociological Review, 41,* 981-992.

Holden, K.C., Burkhauser, R.V. & Feaster, D.J. (1988). The timing of falls into poverty after retirement and widowhood. *Demography, 25,* 405-414.

Holden, K.C., Burkhauser, R.V., & Myers, D.A. (1986). The dynamics of poverty among the elderly: Income transitions at older stages of life. *The Gerontologist, 26,* 292-297.

Holden, K.C. & Smock, P.J. (1991). The economic costs of marital dissolution: Why do women bear a disproportionate cost? *Annual Review of Sociology, 15,* 51-78.

Jensen, L., & McLaughlin, D.K. (1997). The escape from poverty among rural and urban elders. *The Gerontologist, 37,* 462-468.

Jensen, L. & Tienda, M. (1989). Nonmetropolitan minority families in the United States: Trends in racial and ethnic stratification, 1959-1986. *Rural Sociology, 54,* 509-532.

Johnson, K.M. (1989). Recent population redistribution trends in nonmetropolitan America. *Rural Sociology, 54,* 301-326.

Johnson, K.M. (1993). Demographic change in nonmetropolitan America, 1980 to 1990. *Rural Sociology, 58,* 347-365.

Kivett, V.R., & Schwenk, F.N. (1994). The consumer expenditures of elderly women: Racial, marital, and rural/urban impacts. *Journal of Family and Economic Issues, 15,* 261-277.

Lee, G. & Lassey, M.L. (1980). Rural-urban differences among the elderly: Economic, social and subjective factors. *Journal of Social Issues, 36,* 62-74.

Lonsdale, R.E. & Seyler, H.L. (1979). *Nonmetropolitan industrialization.* Washington, DC: V.H. Winston.

McLaughlin, D.K. & Holden, K.C. (1993). Nonmetropolitan elderly women: A portrait of economic vulnerability. *Journal of Applied Gerontology, 12,* 320-334.

McLaughlin, D.K. & Jensen, L. (1993). Poverty among older Americans: The plight of nonmetropolitan elders. *Journals of Gerontology: Social Sciences, 48,* S44-S54.

McLaughlin, D.K., & Jensen, L. (1995). Becoming poor: The experiences of elders. *Rural Sociology. 60,* 202-229.

McLaughlin, D.K. & Jensen, L. (1998). The rural elderly: A demographic portrait. In R.T. Coward and J.A. Krout (Eds.) *Aging in Rural Settings (pp. 15-43).* New York: Springer Publishing.

McLaughlin, D.K., & Perman, L. (1991). Returns versus endowments in the earnings attainment process for metropolitan and nonmetropolitan men and women. *Rural Sociology, 56,* 339-365.

Morgan, L.A. (1991). *After marriage ends: Economic consequences for midlife women.* Newbury Park, CA: Sage.

Olson, L.K. (1994). Women and social security: A progressive approach. *Journal of Aging & Social Policy, 6,* 43-56.

Ozawa, M.N. (1995). The economic status of vulnerable older women. *Social Work, 40,* 323-331.

O'Rand, A.M. (1996). The precious and the precocious: Understanding cumulative disadvantage and cumulative advantage over the life course. *The Gerontologist, 36,* 230-238.

Pienta, A.M., Burr, J.A., & Mutchler, J.E. (1994). Women's labor force participation in later life: The effects of early work and family experiences. *Journal of Gerontology, 49,* S231-S239.

Quadagno, J. (1988). Women's access to pensions and the structure of eligibility rules. *Sociological Quarterly, 29*, 541-558.

Reskin, B.F., & Hartmann, H.I. (1986). *Women's work, men's work: Sex segregation on the job.* Washington, DC: National Academy Press.

Riley, M.W. (1973). Aging and cohort succession: Interpretations and misinterpretations. *Public Opinion Quarterly, Spring,* 35-49.

Ross, C.M., Danziger, S., & Smolensky, E. (1987). Interpreting changes in the economic status of the elderly: 1949-1979. *Contemporary Policy Issues, V*(August), 98-112.

Smeeding, T.M. 1990. Economic status of the elderly. In R.H. Binstock & L.K. George (Eds.) *Handbook of Aging and Social Sciences* (3rd ed.) (pp. 362-381). San Diego: Academic Press.

Smith, K.R., & Moen, P. (1988). Passage through midlife: Women's changing family roles and economic well-being. *Sociological Quarterly, 29*, 503-524.

Tickamyer, A.R., & Bokemeier, J. (1988). Sex differences in labor market experiences. *Rural Sociology, 53*, 166-89.

Tickamyer, A.R., & Duncan, C.M. (1990). Poverty and opportunity structure in rural America. *Annual Review of Sociology, 16*, 67-86.

Warlick, J.L. (1985). Why is poverty after 65 a woman's problem? *Journal of Gerontology, 40*, 751-757.

Zick, C.D., & Smith, K.R. (1986). Immediate and delayed effects of widowhood on poverty: Patterns from the 1970s. *Gerontologist, 26*, 669-675.

Zick, C.D. & Smith, K.R. (1991). Patterns of economic change surrounding the death of a spouse. *Journal of Gerontology: Social Sciences, 46*, S310-S320.

Family Relationships
of Older, Rural Women:
Stability and Change

Jean Pearson Scott, PhD

SUMMARY. The purpose of the study was to examine stability and change in family interaction patterns (availability, interaction, and assistance) of older, rural women as they moved from young-old to late old age. Women (N = 96) were interviewed at two times, twelve years apart. Although there were family network losses, most notably loss of spouse and siblings, family availability and contact showed more stability than change. By late old age, the women were receiving significantly more help from adult children relative to what they gave. Proximity of the adult child was most salient as a predictor of help received from children at both Times 1 and 2. Quality of the adult child relationship was higher for women who received more types of help from adult children at Time 2. The findings suggest that with loss of family members, proximate kin may take up the slack in providing support to rural women of advanced age. *[Article copies available for a fee from The Haworth Document Delivery Service: 1-800-342-9678. E-mail address: getinfo@haworthpressinc.com]*

Family relationships of older women are central to their sense of identity and to the fulfillment of important social roles. They also serve as targets and

Jean Pearson Scott is Professor, Department of Human Development and Family Studies, Texas Tech University, Lubbock, TX 79409.

This study was supported by a grant from the American Association of Family and Consumer Sciences with money generated from the interest portion of the Massachusetts Avenue Building Assets Fund.

[Haworth co-indexing entry note]: "Family Relationships of Older, Rural Women: Stability and Change." Scott, Jean Pearson. Co-published simultaneously in *Journal of Women & Aging* (The Haworth Press, Inc.) Vol. 10, No. 4, 1998, pp. 67-80; and: *Old, Female, and Rural* (ed: B. Jan McCulloch) The Haworth Press, Inc., 1998, pp. 67-80. Single or multiple copies of this article are available for a fee from The Haworth Document Delivery Service [1-800-342-9678, 9:00 a.m. - 5:00 p.m. (EST). E-mail address: getinfo@haworthpressinc.com].

sources of support. Yet, the nature of these relationships in a rural context, particularly the availability and nature of familial interaction in late old age, is not clearly delineated in the extant literature. Accurate perceptions of older, rural women's roles in families and the availability of kin support are unclear because of: (a) the invisible role of older women in comparison to men, particularly in rural environments; (b) the prevalence of myths and stereotypes regarding their status in families; and (c) the lack of comparative studies of older, rural women across multiple rural contexts (Kivett, 1990; McCulloch, 1994).

The marginal status of women, as evidenced by double standards, discrimination, and economic disadvantage, culminates in greater hardships in later life relative to males. In rural areas, women have poorer housing, limited access to medical and social services, and higher rates of poverty in comparison to older, urban women (Kivett, 1997). Concomitantly, the marginality of older, rural women further disadvantages them because they tend to be viewed as a group not worthy of serious study. In rural contexts, traditional gender roles and values continue to predominate and thus males often are regarded as the prime "movers and shakers," and women's family and economic involvements are unrecognized and undervalued.

Older, rural women often are portrayed in contrasting mythical and stereotypical terms–stoic, rugged, and independent or conversely as poor, frail, and dependent (Kivett, 1990). This may be due, in part, to the fact that characteristics of study samples such as region of the country, type of rural locale, ethnic and racial composition, or socioeconomic level are not clearly specified or are ignored as important delimiters in generalizing the findings. The dearth of theoretical underpinning to research, particularly theories that take into account the interplay of persons with their environment, is a limitation of previous research. Also, the lack of data across a variety of rural contexts may contribute to the perpetuation of distorted views of women's roles, the emphasis on their need for support, and the lack of attention to their contributions to the family. Much of the literature on older, rural women, for example, is based on midwestern and southeastern samples (McCulloch, 1994), with virtually no information from the rural southwest.

Much of the literature concerning older, rural women is cross-sectional thereby limiting our understanding of how family relationships change over time (McCulloch, 1994). Not only do we need a time perspective, but one that specifically elucidates the transition from young old age (those years from 65 to 74) to the old and oldest-old age periods. The old (75-84 years of age) and oldest-old (85+ years of age) are presently the largest growing segments of the population. From 1980 to 1990, the number of persons 85 years of age and over increased by nearly 38% to 3 million, an even more rapid increase than the 22% increase in the total older population over the same time period. With greater numbers of old and oldest-old, families will experience extended opportunity for supportive interaction and greater demands for long-term caregiving. Older, rural women may be specifically challenged in maintaining optimal relationships and supportive interaction with their families.

THEORETICAL AND EMPIRICAL BACKGROUND

Person/environment fit theories, such as Lawton and Nahemow's (1973) ecological theory, provide a rationale for considering a person's ability to adjust to changes in later life. Two sources of change, changes in personal competence and environmental changes that occur as one ages in place, such as in a rural environment, are both important to personal well-being. Individuals are constantly engaged in transactions with the environment in order to maintain optimal well-being. In late life, these transactions necessitate accommodations as personal competence factors (health, income) and environmental context changes. Environmental factors are those stimuli possessing some motivating or demand quality for the individual whether the demand is objective or one construed by the individual. Environments have been conceptualized as representing a variety of dimensions, including the personal (e.g., being married and supportive relationships), social (e.g., norms and values), and physical (e.g., crowded versus sparse population density and proximity) (Lawton, 1982). Behavior, whether an outward, observable response or an inner, affective response is an ongoing function of the competence of the person, the press of the environment, and the interaction of the two (see Figure 1).

This perspective has been used by other researchers to examine relocation

FIGURE 1. Adapted from Lawton and Nahemow's Ecological Theory (1973)

Person-Environment Fit Conceptual Model

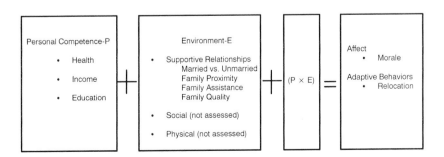

where the assumption was made that out-migration reflected poor person/environment fit (Spitze, Logan, & Robinson, 1992). From these formulations, it was anticipated that in order for older, rural women to maintain good person/environment fit, decrements in personal competence (health, income) and greater environmental press (e.g., loss of spouse) would necessitate compensating or offsetting changes in the environment. As in other studies, information obtained in the sampling efforts described below supported the premise that those women who moved from the area were not able to adequately care for themselves in the existing location and those who aged in place were able to maintain an acceptable person/environment fit.

Family Assistance and Older, Rural Women

An accumulation of research documents the integral involvement of older women with their families as both recipients and providers of instrumental and emotional support and through regular patterns of contact and/or proximal living arrangements. A rural advantage with respect to family interaction and support is often reported; however, caution must be used in rural/urban comparisons and with comparisons across rural locales because significant variations in findings may be overlooked (McCulloch, 1994). With advancing age, rural adults may be more disadvantaged when widowhood is experienced and there are fewer proximate kin in comparison to urban areas.

Older, rural women rate their closeness to kin, particularly adult children and grandchildren, highly and value consensus with them more so than their male counterparts (Dorfman & Mertens, 1990; Powers & Kivett, 1992). Likewise, older, rural women are both greater givers and receivers of instrumental and emotional support than are older, rural men. Proximity to family members appears to be the single most important variable with respect to assistance received from family (Kivett, 1997). Kivett noted that it is not the size of the network, but the number of back-up sources of support that is critical to adequacy of assistance to older, rural women.

Decrements in functional health have implications for the need for support and caregiving. McCulloch (1991) noted little change in rural women's total number of health conditions over a 10-year period, but women's ability to conduct daily activities was notably hindered. In rural areas, most in-home care is provided by family members (Kivett & McCulloch, 1989). The likelihood of detrimental effects of caregiving are greater in rural areas where the lack of and inaccessibility to services, the greater reluctance to use services, and in some areas, greater distance from kin have been documented. The challenges of caregiving in rural environments are further evidenced through the finding that nursing home placements occur at earlier ages on average than in urban environments. Caregiving for a frail husband over an extended period of time may jeopardize the health and well-being of caregiving wives (McCulloch, 1994).

With a few notable exceptions, little research is available regarding the change and stability of family relationships of rural, older women. Kivett and colleagues followed older rural adults over 20 years with 4 waves of data collection (Kivett & McCulloch, 1989; Kivett & Scott, 1976; Kivett & Suggs, 1986; Kivett, Stevenson, Zwane, Cachaper, & Moxley, 1997). The data provide observations about largely female survivors at successive follow-ups over time. At the 20-year follow-up, three-fourths depended upon someone, usually a family member, for regular assistance. Children, most often daughters, provided assistance in the areas of personal care, transportation, home care, medical, and financial management. Perceptions of family support increased with age.

The purpose of the present study was to examine stability and change in family interaction patterns (availability, interaction, and assistance) of rural women as they moved from young old (65 to 74) to late old age (75 and over) from the perspective of a personal competence/environment fit model. The research questions addressed in the study were: What kinds of family interaction and support are available to older, rural women? How does family interaction and support change over time? Are predictors of assistance to young-old predictive of assistance patterns in mid- and late old age?

METHOD

Sample

The sample consisted of 96 women who were interviewed at two times (T1, T2), twelve years apart. The original sample was composed of men and women who were 65 years of age or older in 1981. They were selected from a rural two-county area in the Southwest through use of a compact cluster sampling technique and matched well the demographic profile of the older population in each of the respective counties. Efforts were made to locate the original 571 participants in 1993. Approximately 53% of the original sample was deceased, 24% were interviewed (or their surrogate, n = 8), 21% had moved from the county and could not be located, and 3% refused to participate. Although the percentage of participants who moved was similar to Kivett and McCulloch's (1989) study (18.5%), nearly all movers in the present study relocated outside the county, often at great distance, whereas all of Kivett and McCulloch's movers stayed in the county and were successfully recontacted. This difference reflects the very different circumstances of rural elders. Movers in the present study generally relocated to be in greater proximity to a relative, usually an adult child. With the closest metropolitan area an hour's drive and the next closest one seven hours away, contact often was lost with former community members. Further, there were a number of persons categorized as movers who moved, but were believed to now be deceased. A selection factor was indicated by the fact that movers were less likely to have relatives living in the area at follow-up.

Survivors were younger at T1 than nonsurvivors, however, survivorship was not associated with initial self-reported health. As a crude comparison, national survival statistics indicate that for persons who were 65 years of age in 1980, the approximate time the original data were collected for this study, approximately 24% would be expected to survive to 90 years of age (U.S. Bureau of the Census, 1992). This compares favorably with the response rate of the present study.

At T2, the sample on average was 82.6 years of age (*sd* = 4.5) and had an average educational level of 10.2 years (*sd* = 3.3). The majority were not married (86.1%), and approximately 20% of the T2 sample reported a problem with at least one activity of daily living (ADL) including either bathing, dressing, toileting, walking, incontinence, or feeding. The women rated their overall health at T2 as excellent (24.4%), good (33.3%), fair (34.6%), and poor (7.7%), with less than 20% reporting they had been hospitalized in the preceding six months. Of those who had children, 22.1% saw a child on a daily basis and 20.8% talked to a child on a daily basis. Approximately 35% reported no use of formal services at T2.

Measurement

Demographic variables included *marital status* (married or unmarried) and *education* (the number of years of formal education) (Table 1). *Health* was assessed with a two-item, self-report index. Respondents were asked to rate their present health status from (1) poor to (4) excellent; and perceived change in health over the past 5 years, a variable coded from (1) worse to (3) better. Each item received equal weight (by dividing the item by the number of response codes) and was summed across items for a total score. Cronbach's alpha was .75 at T1 and .65 at T2. *Perceived economic adequacy* was assessed with a three-item index that asked respondents: (a) how satisfied they were with their present standard of living, coded from (1) very dissatisfied to (4) very satisfied; (b) how their income compared to that of others, coded from (1) far below average to (5) far above average; and (c) perceived change in financial situation over the past 5 years, coded from (1) worse to (3) better. Items were weighted equally by dividing each item by its respective answer codes and summing the items for a total score. Cronbach's alphas were .61 and .54 at T1 and T2, respectively.

Structural features of the family network included: number of living chil-

TABLE 1. Background Characteristics of Older, Rural Women at Times 1 and 2

Variables	Time 1	Time 2
Age (M)	70.8(4.5)	82.6(4.5)
Education (M)	10.3(3.2)	10.2(3.3)
Self-Rated Health (M)	1.3(.40)	1.2(.39)*
Perceived Economic Adequacy (M)	2.1(.40)	2.0(.37)
Morale (M)	13.2(2.28)	12.5(2.99)
Marital Status (%)		
Not Married	57.0	86.1
Married	43.0	13.9
Race/Ethnicity (%)		
Anglo	96.2	
Other	3.8	

Note: M = Mean
    Standard Deviations in Parentheses.
*$p < .05$

dren, number of living siblings, proximity of adult children, proximity of siblings, frequency of contact with adult children, frequency of contact with siblings, help received from adult children, help given to adult children, and reciprocity. *Proximity to adult children* and *proximity to siblings* were measured by asking respondents if they had a child and/or sibling living in the household, in the town or neighborhood, within 49 miles, within 50-250 miles, and over 250 miles. Numbers of relatives living at these distances were recorded at T1 and T2. *Frequency of contact* with siblings and adult children was assessed by how often respondents had face-to-face contact with their adult children or siblings at each of the four distances (for relatives in the same household, daily contact was assumed). Possible responses for frequency of contact were: daily, weekly, monthly, several times a year, yearly, and less frequently. When more than one child or sibling lived the same distance from the respondent, the interviewer recorded the one with the highest contact level.

Help received from children and *help given to children* were each measured as a summed 12-item index of different types of assistance provided over the preceding year. Types of assistance included transportation, minor household repairs, housekeeping, shopping, yard work, car maintenance, assistance with illness, important decisions, legal aid, financial aid, and sharing household items and garden produce. Cronbach's alphas for help received from children were .84 and .85 at T1 and T2, respectively. Cronbach's alpha was .78 for help given to children at both T1 and T2. *Reciprocity of assistance,* operationalized as a linear variable, was calculated by subtracting the total number of types of help received from the total number of types of help given to children.

RESULTS

Comparison of the sample at T1 and T2 reflects an older, largely widowed sample with a slight reduction in self-perceived health at T2 (Table 1). Paired t-tests were used to compare means across time on family network characteristics and patterns of assistance variables. With respect to patterns of assistance, older, rural women were receiving more help than twelve years earlier and were giving less help to their adult children (Table 2). Furthermore, the reciprocity of assistance (help given − help received) was less balanced than at T1 (-2.4 vs. -4.7, $p < .001$) (Table 3). That is, older women were now

TABLE 2. Percentage of Older, Rural Women Receiving and Giving Help to Adult Children

Type of Help	Received		Given	
	T1	T2	T1	T2
Transportation	34.3	64.6	14.3	13.6
Household Repairs	48.6	50.8	8.6	3.0
Housekeeping Chores	22.9	32.8	11.4	6.1
Shopping	28.6	54.7	11.4	6.1
Yardwork	29.1	35.4	11.4	3.0
Illness	76.8	75.8	65.7	21.2
Major Decisions	45.7	65.2	25.7	21.2
Legal Aid	17.1	29.2	8.6	3.0
Financial Assistance	14.3	26.2	21.4	9.1
Share Garden Produce	41.4	33.8	34.3	21.2
Share Household Items	24.3	24.6	21.4	16.7
Car Maintenance	34.8	21.5	NA	NA
Other Assistance	14.3	10.0	18.6	11.8

Note: N = 79

TABLE 3. Comparisons over Time for Family Interaction Variables of Older, Rural Women

Type of Help	Time 1	Time 2
Living Spouse	43.0%	13.9%
Number of Living Children	3.2	3.0*
Proximity to Children	2.9	2.9
Frequency of Contact with Child	4.5	4.5
By Proximity		
Town/Neighborhood	5.4	5.4
Within 49 Miles	4.5	4.8
50-250 Miles	3.8	3.5**
Over 250 Miles	2.6	2.8
Help Received From Adult Child	15.8	16.9**
By Proximity		
Town/Neighborhood	17.5	19.5
Within 49 Miles	15.0	15.0
50-250 Miles	16.4	15.5
Over 250 Miles	14.0	14.9
Help Given to Adult Child	13.5	12.3***
Reciprocity (Help Giv-Help Rec)	− 2.4	− 4.7***
Number of Living Siblings	3.5	2.3***
Frequency of Contact w/Siblings	3.6	3.2*
Frequency of Contact w/Siblings		
By Proximity		
Town/Neighborhood (20)	5.3	5.3
Within 49 Miles (6)	4.0	3.5
50-250 Miles (23)	2.7	2.3
Over 250 Miles (32)	1.8	1.8
Proximity to Closest Sibling	2.7	1.8***
Number Living by Proximity		
Town/Neighborhood (12)	1.7	1.3
Within 49 Miles (5)	1.2	1.0
50-250 Miles (24)	2.0	1.6
Over 250 Miles (31)	2.9	1.8**

Note: Paired t-tests were used for all analyses.
*$p < .05$; **$p < .01$; ***$p < .001$

receiving a greater number of different types of assistance and giving fewer types to their adult children than at T1.

Although the mean number of living children had declined significantly (3.2 vs. 3.0, $p < .05$) over time, distance to the most proximate child, had not changed (Table 3). The mean frequency of contact with adult children also had not changed over time; however, when frequency of contact was controlled by proximity, there was significantly less contact with adult children living 50-250 miles away (3.8 vs. 3.5, $p < .01$). Frequency of contact for older women with adult children at other distances remained stable.

Older, rural women had significantly fewer siblings by T2 (3.5 vs. 2.3, $p < .001$) (Table 3). Although mean frequency of contact with siblings had declined, there was a stable pattern of interaction when contact was controlled by proximity of the closest sibling. Loss of siblings had significantly changed the availability of siblings with the closest sibling now living at a greater distance (2.7 vs. 1.8, $p < .001$).

The final question regarding the predictors of help received from adult children was addressed with three regression models, one with T1 variables, the second with T2 variables, and a third with T2 help regressed on T1 predictors (Table 4). The variables entered in the analyses were based on previous literature on the assistance provided by adult children to older parents. Help received from children was regressed on a set of variables entered in a three-step hierarchical regression analysis. Proximity to the adult child was entered first followed by a set of demographic variables (age, education, and marital status). The set of variables entered last in the model included health, relationship quality, and perceived economic adequacy. In the first two regressions (T1 on T1 predictor variables and T2 on T2 predictor variables), help received from adult children was significantly predicted by proximity to child; however, at T2, relationship quality also significantly predicted ($ß = .21$) help received. Older, rural women received more types of help at T2 the closer their child lived to them and the closer they rated their relationship with their adult child.

The final regression analysis was conducted to determine if variables that were significant predictors at T1 continued to explain help received at T2 (Table 4). A technique of analyzing residual change was used whereby T2 help received was regressed first on T1 help received. In this way, only the residual variance was left to be explained by other T1 variables. The residual change in help received is the change that occurs independently of the change that could be predicted on the basis of the initial help received score. Help received at T1 was a significant predictor of help received at T2 and as might be anticipated from T1 results, other T1 variables did not contribute to the model.

TABLE 4. Regression of Help Received from Children on Predictor Variables (N = 66)

Step Variable	T1 on T1 Predictor Variables			T2 on T2 Predictor Variables			T2 on T1 Predictor Variables		
	b	β	R^2	b	β	R^2	b	β	R^2
1 Help Received T1							.54	.38*	.11
1 Prox to Child	1.37	.54***	.29	1.42	.53***	.32			
2 Age	.07	.10		.12	.14				
2 Education	−.12	−.13		−.00	−.00				
2 Married vs. Unmarried	.94	.16	.32	−.27	−.03	.32			
3 Health	.61	.08		−.90	−.11				
3 Rel. Quality	.77	.11		1.14	.21*				
3 Perceived Economic Adeq.	.00	.00	.30	−1.67	−.19	−.38			
	$F_{(4,66)} = 9.16$***			$F_{(7,58)} = 6.63$***			$F_{(1,27)} = 4.50$*		

Note: *$p < .05$; **$p < .01$; ***$p < .001$

DISCUSSION AND CONCLUSIONS

The most striking change in the family relationships of older, rural women in this study was the loss of significant family relationships–loss of husbands, adult children, and siblings. From a person/environmental fit model these losses create greater press and, when coupled with declines in health, reduce the ability of individuals to meet new and existing environmental challenges. The women of this sample appeared to deal with network losses and personal competence declines by mobilizing existing family resources. Indeed, help received from children had increased significantly and patterns of interaction evidenced stability rather than decline across time. For this sample of older, rural women, there appeared to be a "pruning" of the family tree, yet existing family were compensating for network losses through continued visits and increased instrumental assistance. One caveat for the future is that families of these women may have less reserve capacity to deal with future crises or set-backs. Long-term care in rural areas will be crucial for older women and their families when informal back up support is reduced as may be the case for women in late old age.

Higher ratings of closeness to adult children predicted greater types of help received by rural women in late old age (75+ yrs.). This finding is consistent with other literature suggesting that, with age, adult children and parents become more understanding of one another and have fewer areas of conflict (Suitor, Pillemer, Keeton, & Robison, 1994). These mothers may have more positive ratings of their children simply because of the developmental changes that occur over time. Another reason for these positive ratings, however, may be the result of more intensive involvement with proximate daughters and sons. Attachment theory formulations suggest that as parents become more dependent, their children are motivated to care for them and protect them. Thus, relationships motivated by attachment are likely to be evaluated positively.

The perception of the mother only was reported, and so we do not know if the same perception holds for adult children. Walker, Shin, and Bird (1990) found that almost half of mothers reported positive effects of caregiving on the relationship with their adult daughters and, similarly, half of daughters reported positive effects from their caregiving efforts. In the same study, relationship quality was better when caregiving daughters were motivated by love and affection toward their dependent mothers rather than obligation.

The association of relationship quality and greater help received from children is consistent with other literature showing that older, rural widows develop and maintain supportive intimate relationships that aid them through crises (Barer, 1994). In Blackburn, Greenberg, and Boss's (1987) study, investment in children and family and showing strength were frequently mentioned coping mechanisms of rural widows. Similarly, older, rural women showed high levels of affection toward their children and grandchildren (Powers & Kivett, 1992) and, in comparison to rural, older men, had greater exchanges of assistance and association with their children (Atkinson, Kivett, & Campbell, 1986).

This study is limited by a relatively small sample, one geographical location, and limitations in the family measurements that were used. Future studies would benefit from use of qualitative methodologies that provide a different strategy for understanding the meanings of changes in older, rural women's life situations and how these changes are negotiated. Perceptions from the adult child's point of view would be especially insightful in understanding how widowhood, loss of family members, and declines in health change the adult child's relationship with older mothers. Likewise, understanding of how friends and neighbors provide support to women of advanced age could be examined through qualitative methodologies. Another area for future research would be an examination of older women who relocated from the area. For example, one focus might be the identification of factors that were most influential in their relocation decision.

The present study examined family interaction and assistance patterns for a sample of older women from a relatively understudied area of the rural southwest. Despite loss in numbers of kin over a twelve-year period, there was more stability than change in family interaction patterns. Changes were most clearly observed in patterns of assistance where older mothers were receiving greater support from adult children. The tie to proximate kin appeared to be a key factor in maintaining one's independence in this rural environment. For these women of advanced age, aging in place required supportive proximate kin and resilience in the face of adversity.

REFERENCES

Atkinson, M. P., Kivett, V. R., & Campbell, R. T. (1986). Intergenerational solidarity: An examination of a theoretical model. *Journal of Gerontology, 41*, 408-416.

Barer, B. M. (1994). Men and women aging differently. *International Journal of Aging and Human Development, 38*, 29-40.

Blackburn, J. A., Greenberg, J. S., & Boss, P. G. (1987). Coping with normative stress from loss and change: A longitudinal study of rural widows. *Journal of Gerontological Social Work, 21*, 59-70.

Dorfman, L., & Mertens, C. (1990). Kinship relations in retired rural men and women. *Family Relations, 39*, 166-173.

Kivett, V. R. (1990). Older rural women: Mythical, forbearing, and unsung. *Journal of Rural Community Psychology, 11*, 83-101.

Kivett, V. R. (1997). Rural older women. In J. Coyle (Ed.), *Handbook of Women and Aging* (pp. 351-364). Westport, CT: Greenwood.

Kivett, V. R., & McCulloch, B. J. (1989). *Support networks of the very-old: Caregivers and carereceivers (Caswell III).* Final Report to the AARP Andrus Foundation. Greensboro, NC: Family Research Center, School of Human Environmental Sciences, University of North Carolina at Greensboro.

Kivett, V. R., & Scott, J. P. (1976). *The rural by-passed elderly.* Technical Bulletin No. 260. Greensboro, NC: North Carolina Agricultural Research Service, University of North Carolina.

Kivett, V. R., Stevenson, M., Zwane, C., Cachaper, C., & Moxley, S. (1997). *The rural by-passed elderly: 20-year follow-up on the outcomes and needs of the very-old.* Final report to the Retirement Research Foundation. Greensboro, NC: School of Human Environmental Sciences, University of North Carolina at Greensboro.

Kivett, V. R., Suggs, P. (1986). *Caswell revisited: A ten year follow-up on the rural by-passed elderly.* Final report to the AARP Andrus Foundation, Greensboro, NC: Family Research Center, School of Home Economics, University of North Carolina at Greensboro.

Lawton, M. P. (1982). Competence, environmental press, and the adaptation of older people. In M. P. Lawton, P. G. Windley, & T. O. Byerts (Eds.), *Aging and the environment: Theoretical approaches* (pp. 33-59). New York: Springer.

Lawton, M. P., & Nahemow, L. (1973). Ecology and the aging process. In C. Eisdorfer & M. P. Lawton (Eds.), *Psychology of adult development and aging* (pp. 619-674). Washington, DC: American Psychological Association.

McCulloch, B. J. (1991). Health and health maintenance profiles of older rural women, 1976-1986. In A. Bushy (Ed.), *Rural nursing, Vol. I* (pp. 281-296). Newbury Park, CA: Sage.

McCulloch, B. J. (1994). Aging and kinship in rural context. In R. Blieszner & V. H. Bedford (Eds.), *Aging and the family: Theory and research* (pp. 332-354). Westport, CT: Praeger.

Powers, E. A., & Kivett, V. R. (1992). Kin expectations and kin support among rural older adults. *Rural Sociology, 57,* 194-215.

Spitze, G., Logan, J. R., Robinson, J. (1992). Family structure and changes in living arrangements among elderly nonmarried parents. *Journal of Gerontology, 47,* S289-S296.

Suitor, J. J., Pillemer, K., Keeton, S., & Robison, J. (1994). Aged parents and aging children: Determinants of relationship quality. In R. Blieszner and V. H. Bedford (Eds.), *Aging and the family: Theory and research* (pp. 223-242). Westport, CT Greenwood.

U. S. Bureau of the Census (1992). Sixty-five plus in America. *Current Population Reports* (Special Studies, P23-178). Washington, DC: U.S. Government Printing Office.

Walker, A. J., Shin, H., & Bird, D. N. (1990). Perceptions of relationship change and caregiver satisfaction. *Family Relations, 39,* 147-152.

Critical Review:
Synthesis and Recommendations
for Research, Education, and Policy

Vira R. Kivett, PhD

SUMMARY. This paper briefly critiques each of four papers presented at the symposium, relates how these papers contribute additional information on the realities of rural older women, and the implications for future research, policy, and outreach. The critique points out that the realities of rural women's lives can best be understood through their lens in combination with objective observations. Further, most of the conflictual findings in this literature can be attributed to a lack of melding of findings across diverse studies. It is concluded that effective research, policy, and outreach must be predicated on culturally sensitive interpretations of older rural women's realities. *[Article copies available for a fee from The Haworth Document Delivery Service: 1-800-342-9678. E-mail address: getinfo@haworthpressinc.com]*

I have been given the arduous task of deducting logic from inconsistency: "What is the reality of being older, female, and rural?" In other words, can we sort through the myriad data on older rural women, make some sense of it, and move forward with more effective policy and service?

ISSUES OF REALITY

Many issues of older rural women's realities have their origins in views portrayed through historical documents, later reinterpretations of those docu-

---

Vira R. Kivett is Elizabeth Rosenthal Excellence Professor in Human Development and Family Studies, The University of North Carolina at Greensboro, P. O. Box 26170, Greensboro, NC 27402-6170.

[Haworth co-indexing entry note]: "Critical Review: Synthesis and Recommendations for Research, Education, and Policy." Kivett, Vira R. Co-published simultaneously in *Journal of Women & Aging* (The Haworth Press, Inc.) Vol. 10, No. 4, 1998, pp. 81-90; and: *Old, Female, and Rural* (ed: B. Jan McCulloch) The Haworth Press, Inc., 1998, pp. 81-90. Single or multiple copies of this article are available for a fee from The Haworth Document Delivery Service [1-800-342-9678, 9:00 a.m. - 5:00 p.m. (EST). E-mail address: getinfo@haworthpressinc.com].

ments, and more current information obtained from inductive and deductive research (Kivett, 1990, 1997). Our historical fascination with the idealization of rural places has further deferred investigative efforts to understand the reality of rural populations and, especially, older women.

Historically, descriptions of older rural women have been contradictory (Kivett, 1990). While some authors interpreted historical documents to reflect women as reluctant pioneers and passive, later authors, women in particular, provided much more positive portraits. They characterized women as playing vital contributory community and family roles fortified by rich female social networks. More recently, the realities of older rural women have been further confused through the uncompromised findings of qualitative and quantitative research. Collectively, the papers presented here, while methodologically divergent, provide additional information on the realities of older rural women. This symposium demonstrates how the integration of information from varying research methodologies can contribute to more effective advocacy and action for older rural women.

Initially, it is important to recognize that rural women represent a diverse group from small towns, open country, farms, and areas encroaching metropolitan areas (Kivett, 1990). Furthermore, their ethnic backgrounds differ widely. The profile of rural women increasingly changes with influxes of urban retirees, relocated urbanites, migrant workers, and new prototypes of rural dwellers. Many older rural women, however, occupy the same heritage passed on to them by women living off of the land. Vestiges of this inheritance can still be found and are reflected in their dialogued realities. This diversity contributes to some conflictual reports of rural realities. First and foremost, however, is the growing recognition of the need to address older rural women's lives through their lenses.

First, I will briefly critique each of the four papers presented in this symposium; relate how the papers add additional information on the realities of living in a rural place; and discuss implications for future research, policy, and outreach. I will suggest that much of the confusion around the realities of older rural women does not altogether result from the use of different investigative methods, but more importantly, from a lack of synthesis of the findings from this research, namely, qualitative and quantitative studies. Two of the papers report the results of qualitative investigations and two of the presentations are quantitative. Drs. Shenk and Porter used qualitative strategies to examine the realities of older rural women while Drs. McLaughlin and Scott embraced quantitative methodologies.

DR. DENA SHENK'S PAPER

Dr. Shenk, an anthropologist, is known for her sensitive studies of rural women's lives and her rich interpretation of cultural factors influencing their behaviors (e.g., Shenk, 1987, 1991, 1998; Shenk & Christiansen, 1997). Her paper is taken from her well-known database on older rural women in Central Minnesota (Shenk, 1987).

Dr. Shenk examines the subjective realities of aging rural and being female, using the cultural components of life events and personal circumstances to explain behaviors. The thesis of her paper is the importance of understanding a broad range of value based, culturally prescribed perspectives held by rural older women in planning policies and services. Through a field study, or qualitative approach, she presents a case study of one older rural woman, Hilda. Hilda is portrayed as a traditional, rural prototype representing the dualistic reality of most rural women, realities that are both positive and negative. Her methodology includes network analysis to illustrate the rich, culturally prescribed social network that contributed to Hilda's reality. Network analysis, which shows important dimensions of density, intensity, and encapsulation of social networks, is increasingly being used to study the complexity of social networks. Dr. Shenk shows how a rural woman experiences a positive life while living in poverty, poor health, and with many other challenges. Hilda's negotiation of these trials is based upon primary basic values of independence and privacy counterbalanced by a working philosophy regarding the importance of social relationships. Her values are undergirded by feelings of security emanating from a "sense of place" or being "close to the land." Porter later describes this security phenomenon as the desire to stay in familiar surroundings or "close to shore."

Dr. Shenk concludes that Hilda's reality is both positive and negative. While Hilda subjectively interprets objective realities such as economic limitation, social losses, and physical decline, her adaptation is positive. As Dr. Shenk points out, the irony of outcomes is that Hilda's reality is ultimately a contradiction between rural values and aging realities. Although she had strong values of independence, of not accepting formal assistance and relying solely on her informal support she, perhaps, created a more immediate, ultimate, and dependent situation–institutionalization. In this situation, her informal system of support was completely encompassed by a formal system of care.

Several important insights are gained into factors that influence the reality of older rural women: the importance of control over life circumstances; the value of long-standing informal supports; the ability to show continuity in adaptive behavior in the face of life challenges; and the implications of increasing sparseness of social networks and component segregation. Dr. Shenk's research shows the necessity of understanding the intercoiling of older rural women's individual attributes, values, and other perspectives in a provincial setting before developing programs and services to address their needs.

DR. EILEEN PORTER'S PAPER

Dr. Porter's background is nursing. She has made significant contributions to the literature on the life-world of widows (e.g., Porter, 1994, 1995). Her construct of life-world is somewhat synonymous with "reality." She conducts a phenomenological study to explore the life-world of older rural widows and its importance as a context for accessing health care. She defines reality as the result of the individual's interpretation of the boundaries of her life-world (personal shores). For example, poor health is a reality based upon inaccessibility to health care in a familiar locale rather than distance to health care.

Dr. Porter's methodological style is similar to that of Shenk in that it uses reflective dialogues with rural women to observe their subjective reality. It differs from that of Shenk's research, which uses a network analysis approach, by utilizing a prior derived taxonomy of "life-worlds" with which the subjects are classified: feature, or characteristic of the widow's life-world; descriptor, or phrase identifying the feature; and element, or component of the descriptor. Rather than one case study, Porter uses eight subjects. Her study also has a narrower range of outcomes, i.e., access to health care. Furthermore, she examines the subjective reality of older rural women through their use of formal services while Shenk examines informal networks.

The thesis of Dr. Porter's work is the importance of knowing how women, at the center of their world, through their experiences, perceive its parameters which, in turn, influence their realities. For example, many older rural adults like to stay "close to shore" or within familiar locales. Dr. Porter points out that new approaches are needed to more properly interpret problems and to propose solutions that affect the realities of older rural women. What might appear to be a "systems-related" problem such as inadequate transportation to health care may, in fact, be personal resource-environment interaction. That is, access may be related to one's life-world or perceptions of inaccessibility because the care needed is provided outside one's familiar environment. This concept parallels an earlier finding by Shenk (1987). She observed that older rural women reassigned some formal helpers to their informal, familiar networks, a way of legitimizing their acceptance of formal support. Thus, the reality of older rural women's support systems may, in part, hinge on culturally and personally defined familiarity. Other common factors impacting and problematic to the parameters of shore include specialty and technological health care, telecommunications, social interaction, discount purchasing, energy levels, and locally unavailable products.

Several important insights are gained from Porter's investigation into factors influencing the realities of older rural women: (a) rural values equate acceptance with familiarity which has important implications for health access, the marketplace, and social interaction; (b) there is a "family shared" sense of shore with important implications for informal support systems; and (c) definitions of "shore," or "the familiar" are unique to each woman. Dr. Porter's research shows the experiences of older rural persons to be vital resources of knowledge in their access to products and services, in providing new approaches to labeling problems, and in proposing solutions. Dr. Porter is explicit in her concern for the continuing practice of relying on system-related factors such as distance, use, and barriers as indicators of service access rather than the use of cultural contextual factors.

DR. DIANE MCLAUGHLIN'S PAPER

Dr. Diane McLaughlin is a rural sociologist and, as such, typifies the use of traditional quantitative methodologies in explaining life outcomes or realities. She has made significant contributions to the literature on the economic realities of metropolitan and, particularly, nonmetropolitan elders (e.g., McLaughlin & Holden, 1993; McLaughlin & Jensen, 1993, 1995, 1998; McLaughlin & Perman, 1991).

In her paper, Dr. McLaughlin shows the economic realities of older rural women through comparative analyses of cohorts of metro and nonmetro women and through changes in their economic status over time. She determines if the factors associated with the economic realities of nonmetro older women differ from those of older metro women. She points out the variable economic realities of women according to region, education, marital status, rurality, age cohort, and ethnicity. Dr. McLaughlin explains these variations in realities as resulting from cohort effects or socio-historical events. She employs cohort analyses using both descriptive and inferential statistics, most notably multiple regression analysis. Other than her quantitative approach in examining older women's realities, her research differs from the investigations of Shenk and Porter in sample size, the secondary nature of her database, the use of statistical analyses, and generalizability. By its nature, her research allows for a more precise estimate of the variance explained in the realities of older women than the qualitative studies and it allows for predictability. The results of her analyses of the predictors of the economic reality of older women show that, although honorable, no more than one-third of the variation in the economic reality of metro and nonmetro women is explained by her research model. Furthermore, her analyses show the economic reality of older metro women can be predicted better than that of corresponding rural women. On the other hand, the subjective, micro-investigations of Shenk and Porter raise inherent questions of representation.

McLaughlin's work provides insights into the realities of nonmetro older women: cohort fluctuations in economic realities can be traced to socio-historical influences and to selection bias from mortality; and the metro/nonmetro gap (favoring metro women) will continue to widen in the future because of persisting rural disadvantages in earnings, pension coverage, and job access. Dr. McLaughlin's research shows that birth cohort and residence have important impacts on the economic realities of older women. Her results strongly suggest the need to consider the development of policies and programs that are sensitive to fluctuations in the economic realities between cohorts and the persisting negative effects of living in a rural area. In particular, her findings suggest the need to address the objective economic realities of rural women, such as those related to race, marital status, and family size.

DR. JEAN SCOTT'S PAPER

Dr. Scott is in the field of Human Development and Family Studies. She is recognized for her work in generational and intergenerational relationships and social supports, especially among older rural adults (e.g., Scott, 1996; Scott & Caldwell, 1996; Scott & Roberto, 1987; Scott, Roberto, & Hutton, 1986). Dr. Scott's regional study addresses older rural women's reality of informal social support. Her research design, similar to that of McLaughlin, is of the quantitative type incorporating both descriptive and inferential statistics. It examines the informal social support realities of rural women over time. Her research, although quantitative, differs from that of Dr. McLaughlin. Although both studies examine change in and prediction of older rural women's realities, Dr. Scott's study is theoretically driven and follows the same group of women over time. Her use of personal competence/environmental fit model seems especially appropriate given Dr. Shenk's and Porter's premises of the importance of environmental influences to life outcomes. This perspective states that actions are the results of personal ability, the forces in one's surroundings, and the interaction of the two. This viewpoint, although theoretically conjected, parallels and further supports the findings of Drs. Shenk and Porter which show the importance of personal characteristics and cultural context to women's realities. In contrast to the latter two studies, Dr. Scott bases her interpretations on system-related phenomena rather than on the context of a personal environment interaction. Moreover, the profile of her sample of 96 rural women reflected the population profile for that subgroup, thus contributing to the study's generalizability.

Dr. Scott's data show that older rural women's realities relative to their psychological well-being (morale) and economic well-being are stable over time. This finding persists despite older women's perceptions of health changes. These data demonstrate changes in several structures affecting rural women's social support. For example, there is a significant drop over time in number of living children and in frequency of contact with primary children living at a distance. Similarly, there are decreases in reciprocal exchanges by older women, e.g., less giving, more receiving from children. Similar changes are detected for relations with siblings. The most consistent predictor of assistance from children over time is proximity. Hence, the reality of child assistance, a primary source, continues to be hinged on distance. Given Porter's concern that such findings are interpreted in a person-environment interaction context rather than in a system-focused one, however, presents questions regarding Dr. Scott's interpretation. Is the importance of distance to a child explained pragmatically or through a nearest to shore explanation? Hence, Dr. Scott's results show the reality of older rural women's social support system is that help from children increases in the occurrence of decreasing numbers of primary and secondary kin. This reality occurs in the context of decreased reciprocity between older women and their families.

IMPLICATIONS

Implications for Clarifying Realities

The rich and assorted findings from the diverse studies presented here could add further confusion in understanding the realities of older rural women. Yet, a close look at research outcomes suggests the complementary nature of the studies. Much of the mythical nature of realities has come about because of a lack of appropriate synthesis of findings. The rich insightful data from qualitative studies can be intricately and vitally woven into quantitative findings. This process, in turn, can contribute to more accurate and appropriate uses of research findings. Examples of this possible convergence of findings can be seen in several instances. Porter's use of the life-world concept may have implications for the interpretation of Scott's finding regarding the importance of proximity to informal support access. That is, the relationship between proximity of children and help received may be based upon a person-environment explanation rather than a system-related one. Similarly, Shenk's observation of the ability of rural women to adjust to personal changes may be reflected in Scott's finding that the morale of older rural women did not change over time despite potentially damaging changes in reciprocal helping patterns. McLaughlin's finding of the importance of marital status to the economic reality of women is visible through Shenk and Porter's observations of the social and economic challenges faced by older widowed women. Other such examples of this interweaving of findings could be cited.

Implications for Future Research

The results of this symposium show the importance of combining investigative methods in constructing the life realities of older rural women. The richness of rural women's heritage, the cultural context of their aging process, and their complex lives require other than singular, linear explanations. Qualitative data can inform research paradigms and the interpretation of realities. Efforts should be made to make the investigative content of qualitative and quantitative studies more complementary to assist in the synthesis of findings from the two data types. Methodologies are needed that will facilitate the operationalization of network analyses in quantitative research to capture the multidimensionality of the realities of women's lives. Specifically, future quantitative research on older rural women should produce predictive models that explain a larger portion of the variation in older rural women's outcomes than present models. This process may involve a greater convergence of theoretical models which use constructs derived from qualitative studies. Increasingly, research must be designed and interpreted in the context of "the rural perspective" to better inform policy. More information is needed on the intricacy of the support networks of older rural women. Greater use of network analyses undergirded by better defined models of density, intensity, and other network qualities is needed to interpret the richness of rural support systems.

Implications for Policy and Outreach

McLaughlin's work points out the inherent problems in using public databases such as census data when policy, or its lack there of, leads to inconsistencies in census data formats across time. Furthermore, data need to be in easily assessable forms amenable to modification to represent the realities of obscured aging groups.

Qualitative data in combination with quantitative data, increasingly viewed as a desirable convergence, can sensitize policy makers to the realities of older rural populations. As noted by Shenk, policy makers often look at statistics rather than exploring the complex views of actual individuals. Her findings and those of Porter show that it is through rural elders' eyes that appropriate programs and services can be developed most effectively to meet their needs. Results of Scott and McLaughlin's studies underscore the importance of longitudinal and cohort analyses in examining the life realities of older rural women. These data mesh well with the qualitative observations by Shenk on adaptability and continuity in the lives of rural women.

Data presented by Porter suggest the caution to be exercised in policy and outreach for rural populations, namely acting on system-related interpretations only. As she noted, if certain phenomena are interpreted in the context of a person-environment interaction, that is, how individuals subjectively view access to services, problems may be better identified and proposed solutions more effective than relying only on a system-related or a functional interpretation such as geographical distance.

It is important that policy developers respond to the needs of older rural women within their cultural contexts. Policy makers must respond to older rural women's needs by understanding their cultural values, respecting independence, privacy, and primary dependence upon natural support systems. They should also enhance the supportive contributions of network members beyond that of the primary family such as secondary and fictive kin and important attenuated helpers. The important concept of "familiarity" or "near shore" found among rural populations should guide policy addressing location of services. Policy makers must continue to strive to enhance work opportunities and benefits (including pensions and other retirement benefits) in rural areas. These efforts will have the overall effects of strengthening network support systems and the individual resources of older rural adults, especially those of future cohorts. Lastly, similar to means tests, policies should be developed that are flexible enough to address older cohort differences in personal resources.

Outreach must respect but be proactive in the linking of informal and formal networks of older rural women to delay or prevent institutionalization. Service developers must become more aware that issues of older rural women are issues of the family such as distance to medical care and other needed resources. This need is exemplified by Scott's research. Education is needed to maintain intergenerational harmony in the face of decreasing reciprocity among older rural women and their families. Additionally, the remarkable strengths of rural women as viewed over time can be used in the development of community programs; advocacy for weaker, more vulnerable peers; and in the expansion and strengthening of services and helping networks.

Finally, accumulating data on the life outcomes of older rural women are less in conflict when data from various sources and different methodologies are compared and synthesized. Problems of clarity in findings across studies have occurred primarily as a function of a lack of synthesis of findings, clarity of method, and diversity of samples. Qualitative and quantitative research can benefit from the strengths and weaknesses of each research strategy. Whether both strategies are incorporated into the same study or findings across studies are integrated, resulting interpretations will contribute to more culturally relevant and effective research, policy, and outreach.

REFERENCES

Kivett, V. R. (1990). Older rural women: Mystical, forebearing, and unsung. *Journal of Rural Community Psychology, 2,* 83-101.

Kivett, V. R. (1997). Rural older women. In J. M. Coyle (Ed.). *Handbook on women and aging* (pp. 351-364). Westport, CT: Greenwood Publishing.

McLaughlin, D. K., & Holden, K. C. (1993). Nonmetropolitan elderly women: A portrait of economic vulnerability. *Journal of Applied Gerontology, 12,* 320-334.

McLaughlin, D. K., & Jensen, L. (1993). Poverty among older Americans: The plight of nonmetropolitan elders. *Journals of Gerontology: Social Sciences, 48,* S44-S54.

McLaughlin, D. K., & Jensen, L. (1995). Becoming poor: The experiences of elders. *Rural Sociology, 60,* 202-229.

McLaughlin, D. K., & Jensen, L. (1998). The rural elderly: A demographic portrait. In R. T. Coward & J. A. Krout (Eds.), *Aging in rural settings* (pp.15-43). New York: Springer.

McLaughlin, D. K., & Perman, L. (1991). Returns versus endowments in the earnings attainment process for metropolitan and nonmetropolitan men and women. *Rural Sociology, 56,* 339-365.

Porter, E. J. (1994). Older widows' experience of living alone at home. *Image: Journal of Nursing Scholarship, 26,* 19-24.

Porter, E. J. (1995). The life-world of older widows: The context of lived experience. *Journal of Women & Aging, 7*(4), 31-46.

Scott, J. P. (1996). Sisters in later life: Changes in contact and availability. *Journal of Women & Aging, 8*(3-4), 41-53.

Scott, J. P., & Caldwell, J. (1996). Needs and program strengths: Perceptions of Hospice volunteers. *The Hospice Journal, 11*(1), 19-30.

Scott, J. P., & Roberto, K. A. (1987). Informal supports of older adults: A rural-urban comparison. *Family Relations, 36,* 444-449.

Scott, J. P., Roberto, K. A., & Hutton, J. T. (1986). Families of Alzheimer's victims: Family support to the caregivers. *Journal of the American Geriatrics Society, 34,* 348-354.

Shenk, D. (1987). *Someone to lend a helping hand–the lives of rural older women in Central Minnesota.* St. Cloud, MN: Central Minnesota Council on Aging.

Shenk, D. (1991). Older rural women as recipients and providers of social support. *Journal of Aging Studies, 5,* 347-358.

Shenk, D. (1998). *Someone to lend a helping hand: Women growing older in rural America.* Gordon and Breach.

Shenk, D., & Christiansen, K. (1997). Social support systems of rural older women: A comparison of the U.S. and Denmark. In J. Sokolovsky (Ed.), *The cultural context of aging: Worldwide perspectives* (2nd Ed.) (pp. 331-349). Greenwood.

Epilogue

B. Jan McCulloch, PhD

One of the primary premises for this volume was the importance of understanding the conflicting images often presented regarding the experiences of women growing old in rural settings. As these papers have shown, when taken separately, images might appear to be conflicting. As an integrated set of papers examining multiple aspects of rural women's lives, however, they more clearly point to the complexity of the aging experiences of this diverse group of women. Three important conclusions regarding this complexity can be drawn.

First, the aging experiences of rural women must be viewed as diverse. Shenk's case study underscores the historical characteristics of rural residents. Hilda was stoic about her situation, she spoke frequently about the importance of remaining independent as long as possible, and she identified the linkages she had with family and friends in her community. Hilda's aging experience, however, was affected by the deaths of both of her sons. The effect of these deaths cannot be underestimated when seen in the context of Scott's results showing the importance of proximate children to reciprocity. Without proximate family members, Hilda was unable to care for herself after the death of her husband, and she relocated to an institutional setting–a place where she never felt at home. Additionally, the recurring financial hardship theme in Hilda's life review is supportive of McLaughlin's results comparing the economic well-being of rural women to their urban counterparts. Although positive about her life, Hilda frequently spoke of the economic difficulties that consistently accompanied her childhood, adulthood, and old age.

B. Jan McCulloch is Associate Professor, Department of Family Studies and Sanders-Brown Center on Aging, University of Kentucky, Lexington, KY 40506-0054.

[Haworth co-indexing entry note]: "Epilogue." McCulloch, B. Jan. Co-published simultaneously in *Journal of Women & Aging* (The Haworth Press, Inc.) Vol. 10, No. 4, 1998, pp. 91-93; and: *Old, Female, and Rural* (ed: B. Jan McCulloch) The Haworth Press, Inc., 1998, pp. 91-93. Single or multiple copies of this article are available for a fee from The Haworth Document Delivery Service [1-800-342-9678, 9:00 a.m. - 5:00 p.m. (EST). E-mail address: getinfo@haworthpressinc.com].

Second, these studies once again underscore the importance of family and community ties in the lives of women aging in rural settings. Scott's results are particularly important in this regard. The reciprocity that often has described rural community life continues to be important as women age, even though there are shifts in the balance of this reciprocity. Her data show that rural families, as historically indicated, continue to be supportive to their older family members. Importantly, however, Scott notes that this support for rural elders might necessitate a relocation from life-long residences. As younger family members leave rural areas for better employment opportunities, older women may find it necessary to leave friends, communities, and long-time social networks to be near proximate support—often to communities that are more urban than those experienced during a lifetime of rural living. When Scott's results are paired with those of McLaughlin, implications for social and economic well-being are identifiable. Compared with urban women, those aging in rural environments are more likely to experience economic hardship with age—especially if they are widowed, separated, or divorced. In addition, it is possible that they may relocate and leave behind well established social support and friendship networks.

Third, Porter's identification of person-centered reasons for accessing services and health care provide an avenue for understanding why rural women, often in poorer health than women aging in urban areas, are less likely to utilize these services. Her dialogues with older rural women provide an understanding of rural women's interpretations of rural and urban environments. Distance meant little to some; one resident traveled approximately 90 miles to her previous community to obtain care from familiar providers. Rural women with experience in larger communities were not as hesitant to travel to urban areas for care—their personal shores were expandable. Others who were more life-long rural residents were less likely to seek help in urban areas; their shores were more narrow. These results, combined with those of the other contributors, support the complexity of women aging in rural spaces. In addition, McLaughlin's cohort analyses suggest that, in the future, the economic well-being of rural women might not improve or might not improve at the same rate as their urban counterparts.

In conclusion, these papers cannot clarify the conflicting images of older rural women. Some, indeed, can be characterized as stoic, independent, and deeply rooted in family and community. The older women viewed up close and personal in the two qualitative studies provide insights regarding the strengths of these characteristics for some. Additionally, some rural women demonstrate their capacity for adaptability—a characteristic that assists them with decisions about when and where they will relocate when the need arises. In more general terms, rural women are more likely to be economically disadvantaged than their urban counterparts, but they also grow older within families where reciprocity remains important. The images, depending upon the lens and the focus of inquiry, remain; depth of understanding is developed from our ability to overlay the many images that are contained as we examine the lives of women aging in rural settings.

Index

[*Note:* Page numbers followed by f indicate figures; page numbers followed by t indicate tables.]

Aday, L.A., 26-28,37
Advantages, of older rural women,
  12-14
Adversity, of older rural women,
  12-14
African Americans, older rural
  women, economic realities
  of, 45-46
Aging, of older rural women,
  adaptations of, 15-17
Andersen, R.M., 26-28,37

Bird, D.N., 78
Blackburn, J.A., 78
Boss, P.G., 78
Breast cancer, in older rural women, 2
Buss, T.F., 37

Campbell, R.T., 43
Cancer, breast, in older rural women,
  2
Cohort succession, in economic
  well-being of elders, 42-43
Community roles, of older rural
  women, 2
Community ties, of older rural
  women, 2
Coward, R.T., 27
Crystal, S., 43,51

Economic issues, of older rural
  women, 41-65. *See also*

Rural women, older,
  economic realities of
Education, in economic well-being
  of elders, 43-44
Employment opportunities, for older
  rural women, 1
Environment, as factor in family
  relationships of older rural
  women, 69,69f

Family assistance, and older rural
  women, 70-71
Family relationships, of older rural
  women, 2,67-80
  study of, 71-74
    discussion, 77-79
    measurement in, 72-74,73t
    results, 74-76,74t,75t,77t
    sample in, 71-72
Formal structures, older rural
  women's views of, 9-10
Friendship networks, of older rural
  women, 2,8

Gillanders, W.R., 37
Greenberg, J.S., 78

Health care, use by older rural
  widows, 25-39. *See also*
  Rural widows, older, health
  care use by
Henretta, J.C., 43
Hicks, L., 27

Haworth
DOCUMENT DELIVERY
SERVICE

This valuable service provides a single-article order form for any article from a Haworth journal.

- *Time Saving:* No running around from library to library to find a specific article.
- *Cost Effective:* All costs are kept down to a minimum.
- *Fast Delivery:* Choose from several options, including same-day FAX.
- *No Copyright Hassles:* You will be supplied by the original publisher.
- *Easy Payment:* Choose from several easy payment methods.

Open Accounts Welcome for . . .
- Library Interlibrary Loan Departments
- Library Network/Consortia Wishing to Provide Single-Article Services
- Indexing/Abstracting Services with Single Article Provision Services
- Document Provision Brokers and Freelance Information Service Providers

---

MAIL or *FAX* THIS ENTIRE ORDER FORM TO:

Haworth Document Delivery Service
The Haworth Press, Inc.
10 Alice Street
Binghamton, NY 13904-1580

or FAX: 1-800-895-0582
or CALL: 1-800-429-6784
9am-5pm EST

PLEASE SEND ME PHOTOCOPIES OF THE FOLLOWING SINGLE ARTICLES:

1) Journal Title: _____
   Vol/Issue/Year:_____ Starting & Ending Pages:_____
   Article Title:_____
   _____

2) Journal Title: _____
   Vol/Issue/Year:_____ Starting & Ending Pages:_____
   Article Title:_____
   _____

3) Journal Title: _____
   Vol/Issue/Year:_____ Starting & Ending Pages:_____
   Article Title:_____
   _____

4) Journal Title: _____
   Vol/Issue/Year:_____ Starting & Ending Pages:_____
   Article Title:_____
   _____

(See other side for Costs and Payment Information)

COSTS: Please figure your cost to order quality copies of an article.

1. Set-up charge per article: $8.00
   ($8.00 × number of separate articles) _____
2. Photocopying charge for each article:

   1-10 pages: $1.00 _____

   11-19 pages: $3.00 _____

   20-29 pages: $5.00 _____

   30+ pages: $2.00/10 pages _____

3. Flexicover (optional): $2.00/article _____
4. Postage & Handling: US: $1.00 for the first article/
   $.50 each additional article _____

   Federal Express: $25.00 _____

   Outside US: $2.00 for first article/
   $.50 each additional article _____

5. Same-day FAX service: $.50 per page _____

   GRAND TOTAL: _____

METHOD OF PAYMENT: (please check one)

❏ Check enclosed ❏ Please ship and bill. PO # _____
   (sorry we can ship and bill to bookstores only! All others must pre-pay)

❏ Charge to my credit card: ❏ Visa; ❏ MasterCard; ❏ Discover;
   ❏ American Express;

Account Number: _____ Expiration date: _____

Signature: *X* _____

Name: _____ Institution: _____

Address: _____

_____

City: _____ State: _____ Zip: _____

Phone Number: _____ FAX Number: _____

MAIL or *FAX* THIS ENTIRE ORDER FORM TO:

Haworth Document Delivery Service	**or FAX:** 1-800-895-0582
The Haworth Press, Inc.	**or CALL:** 1-800-429-6784
10 Alice Street	(9am-5pm EST)
Binghamton, NY 13904-1580